Two-Bite Cupcakes

An Imagine Book
Published by Charlesbridge
85 Main Street, Watertown, MA 02472
617-926-0329
www.charlesbridge.com

Created by Penn Publishing Ltd.
1 Yehuda Halevi Street, Tel Aviv, Israel 65135
www.penn.co.il

Design and layout: Michal & Dekel
Culinary editor & styling: Deanna Linder
Photography by Danya Weiner

Library of Congress
Cataloging-in-Publication Data

Goren, Viola.
Two-bite cupcakes / Viola Goren.
        p. cm.
ISBN 978-1-936140-14-5
(hardcover: alk. paper)
1.Cupcakes. I. Title.
TX771.G643 2010
641.8'653--dc22
            2010001631
2 4 6 8 10 9 7 5 3

For information about custom editions, special sales, premium and corporate purchases,
please contact Charlesbridge Publishing, Inc. at specialsales@charlesbridge.com

Two-Bite Cupcakes

Viola Goren

Photography by Danya Weiner

imagine!
Publishing

Contents

Introduction

Bite size cupcakes are all the rage these days, and rightfully so. With the abundance of classic and exotic flavors available, who can resist trying them all? That's where mini cupcakes come in. The mini cupcake is literally a two-bite treat, meaning you can have a few without feeling the guilt. This book will explore the countless ways you can bake and decorate these fabulous petite treats.

In the first chapter, Cupcake Essentials, you will find a list of all the necessary tools and main ingredients needed to make these two-bite cupcakes.

In the second chapter, Basic Frosting Recipes, I've provided the recipes for all of the frostings used in the book. Follow the recipes to a tee and you'll produce delicious delights; or be creative and use the recipes as a base, adding your own favorite ingredients.

From the outside, cupcakes appear to be all about the frosting. But in the third chapter, It's in the Filling, you'll find many recipes that prove otherwise. From luscious creams to crunchy nuts and sweet fruits, these sweet treats provide a surprise in every bite.

What would a cupcake be without its topping? The fourth chapter, It's in the Topping, provides numerous recipes for special toppings that will suit all ages and tastes. For the kids, you can't go wrong with the Oreo Cupcakes or the Cola Cupcakes, and for the older crowd try serving the Crème Brulée or Plum Cobbler Cupcakes at your next party.

Chocolate lovers beware—in the fifth chapter, Nothing but Chocolate, you'll have a hard time choosing between classic chocolate treats (like the Chocolate Soufflé Cupcakes) and more adventurous recipes (like the Nutella Surprise Cupcakes).

Traditionally, cupcakes are thought of as sweet treats. But in chapter six, It's Gotta be Savory, you'll find a variety of recipes for bite size savory bakes that work not only as delectable appetizers but also as great afternoon snacks.

And finally, the recipes in the last chapter, Time for Celebration, will add an out-of-the-ordinary touch to your next holiday or birthday bash. Your guests will be delightfully surprised by the creatively decorated and equally tasty mini desserts.

Cupcake Essentials

Equipment

Most of the basic tools for cupcake baking can be found in the average kitchen. Some of the more professional tools, such as thermometers and scales, will serve you well in all your baking and cooking endeavors, and it's worth investing in them.

CUPCAKE PANS I recommend using a 24-cup mini cupcake pan, metal or Teflon, for the recipes in this book. Make sure to line the pans with mini cupcake liners before baking. For the savory cupcakes, I suggest using a 24-cup Silicon mini cupcake pan, which eliminates the need for liners.

MEASURING TOOLS Baking is an exact science, and the proportions of one ingredient to another are crucial. This is why I recommend working with measuring tools such as digital scales and standard measuring cups, teaspoons, and tablespoons. Liquid ingredients should be measured in transparent measuring cups with spouts and clear markings at ¼-cup intervals. Metal measuring cups are best for dry ingredients.

OVEN Any type of oven can be used to bake mini cupcakes. Since not every oven functions in the same way, however, you must relate to the baking times and temperatures as approximations, adjusting them as needed. If you need to alter the baking times significantly in your oven, you may want to consider purchasing an oven thermometer or having your oven recalibrated.

PASTRY BAGS AND DECORATING TIPS Also known as piping bags, pastry bags can be purchased at specialty cooking shops, along with an assortment of matching tips. If your recipe calls for a pastry bag but you choose not to make a special design, you can fill an average-size zip-lock bag with your favorite topping, cut a hole in one corner, and pipe away! Decorating tips come in various sizes and shapes, allowing for a vast choice of designs.

STAND MIXER Most of the recipes in this book call for a stand mixer fitted with either a whisk or paddle attachment. If you really love to bake, I encourage you to buy a heavy-duty stand mixer. They may be a bit expensive, but they are nearly indestructible and will last a lifetime. If you don't have a stand mixer, a hand electric mixer will do. I do not suggest hand whisking, however.

TIMER Exact timing is essential in baking, so be sure to have a timer on hand.

WIRE COOLING RACK Once baked, cupcakes must be cooled to prevent steam from collecting at the bottom of the pan. The moisture will turn the base of the cupcakes damp and spongy.

Ingredients

BUTTER None of the recipes here that call for butter should be made with a butter substitute! The best butter to use is unsalted; if you can't find it, use salted. When a recipe calls for very cold butter, it should be just that. You'll taste the difference in the finished product.

DECORATIONS The sky's the limit nowadays when it comes to decorating baked goods. Be as creative as you wish, making use of fruit, colorful candy, chocolates of various sizes, colored sugar, and any other garnish that adds color and fun to a cupcake. Make sure the adornments you select are edible, and store them in a dry, dark place to prevent their color from fading.

EGGS Eggs make the texture of the cupcake batter richer and help bind ingredients together. It's best to use fresh, medium-size eggs that are at room temperature.

FLOUR Nearly all recipes in the book call for all-purpose flour. To measure, scoop it out of a flour bag or jar using a measuring cup so that the flour mounts over the top of the cup. Sweep the back of a knife across the top of the measuring cup to level the flour. All types of flour should be stored in tightly sealed containers (I like wide ones for easy scooping) in a cool, dry cupboard.

HEAVY CREAM Also called whipping cream, heavy cream should have a milk fat content of 35-40%. Always store heavy cream in the refrigerator until use, since very cold cream produces the best results.

SUGAR The sugar to use for these recipes is granulated, unless another (brown, powdered or confectioners') is mentioned. All sugar should be stored in tightly sealed containers in a cool, dry cupboard.

SUGAR DOUGH Sugar dough is available for purchase in various colors or in white. Food coloring is often added when using the dough for decoration.

Basic Recipes

Crème Fraiche

Makes 4 cups

Homemade crème fraiche is really easy to make and great to have on hand. For all the recipes in this book calling for crème fraiche, you can substitute with the same amount of sour cream or buttermilk.

Ingredients
3 cups heavy cream
1 cup sour cream

Preparation
1. In a medium bowl, mix the heavy cream and sour cream. Transfer mixture to a clean glass jar, cover with plastic wrap and let sit at room temperature for 24 hours.
2. After 24 hours, mix and transfer to the refrigerator. May be kept refrigerated for up to two weeks.

Pastry Cream

Makes 4 cups

Also known as crème patisserie or vanilla cream, this frosting can be used as the base for any pastry cream.

Ingredients
2 cups whole milk
1 teaspoon pure vanilla extract
1 cup sugar
7 egg yolks
3 teaspoons cornstarch
3 teaspoons all-purpose flour
¾ stick (3 oz.) butter

Preparation
1. In a medium saucepan, bring the milk and vanilla extract to a boil.
2. In a medium bowl, mix the sugar, egg yolks, cornstarch, and flour.
3. Pour ⅓ of the milk and vanilla mixture into the egg yolk mixture, stirring constantly. Gradually pour the milk and egg mixture into the saucepan, stirring constantly.
4. Cook on a low flame, still stirring, until the cream thickens, 5-7 minutes.
5. Remove from the heat, stir to cool a bit, and add the butter.
6. Cover well with plastic wrap and refrigerate for up to four days.

Variations
+ Add a teaspoon of cinnamon or ground coffee to the sugar.
+ Add a teaspoon of your favorite liqueur before adding the butter.
+ Replace the pure vanilla extract with a vanilla bean.

Swiss Meringue Frosting

Makes 4 cups

This light and fluffy frosting doesn't overpower the taste of the cupcake itself and works great for piping shapes.

Ingredients
1 cup egg whites
(from about 8 large eggs)

2 cups sugar

Preparation
1. Place the egg whites and sugar in a heatproof bowl. Set the bowl over a saucepan of gently simmering water and stir occasionally, until the sugar dissolves. Remove the bowl from the pan.
2. Using a stand mixer fitted with a whisk attachment, place the egg white and sugar mixture in the bowl and whisk until the egg whites have cooled and become firm.

Variations
+ For a fancy look, brown the frosting with a kitchen torch.
+ Add the zest of one lemon or half an orange to the eggs whites and sugar before simmering.
+ Add a teaspoon of cacao to the egg whites and sugar in the mixer.

Royal Icing

Makes 1 cup

This delicate frosting is great for cupcakes that need only a touch of sweetness on top.

Ingredients
1 tablespoon water
1 cup powdered sugar

Preparation
1. In a bowl, whisk the water and powdered sugar.
2. Continue whisking until the mixture reaches a paste-like consistency.

Variations
+ Replace the tablespoon of water with a tablespoon of any fruit juice (lemon, orange, cranberry, apple, etc.) for a more colorful and flavorful icing.

Swiss Meringue Buttercream

Makes 4 cups

All the pleasure of the Swiss Meringue Frosting (see page 15), with the creaminess of butter.

Ingredients
1 cup egg whites
(from about 8 large eggs)

2 cups sugar
2 teaspoons pure vanilla extract
4 sticks (16 oz.) butter, cut into cubes

Preparation
1. Place the egg whites and sugar in a heatproof bowl. Set the bowl over a saucepan of gently simmering water and stir occasionally, until the sugar dissolves and the mixture smooth. Remove the bowl from the pan.
2. Place the egg white mixture in a bowl and using a stand mixer with a whisk attachment, whisk until the egg whites cool.
3. Gradually whisk in the vanilla extract and butter.
4. May be stored in the refrigerator for up to two weeks.

Variations
+ Add 8 oz. of melted dark chocolate (cooled) after adding the vanilla extract and butter.
+ Add the zest and juice of one lemon during the first step for a tangy, creamy flavor.
+ Replace the vanilla extract with quality maple syrup.

Cream Cheese Frosting

Makes 2 cups

The easiest of all to make, this creamy and tangy frosting is a great complement to a sweet cupcake.

Ingredients
1 cup (8 oz.) cream cheese
1 cup powdered sugar
1 teaspoon lemon juice
1 tablespoon heavy cream

Preparation
1. Using a stand mixer fitted with a paddle attachment, mix the cream cheese and powdered sugar until fluffy and light in color.
2. Add the lemon juice and heavy cream and mix to incorporate the ingredients.

Variations
+ Replace the lemon juice with 2 tablespoons of honey for a rich, sweet flavor.
+ Replace the lemon juice with one tablespoon of fresh squeezed orange
+ Replace the lemon juice with 1 tablespoon of instant espresso powder.

Whipped Ganache Frosting

Makes 3 cups

It is very important to chill the chocolate and heavy cream mixture after cooking so that it whips properly. Also, use a quality dark chocolate containing over 60% cacao.

Ingredients
1 cup heavy cream
10 oz. dark chocolate

Preparation
1. In a small saucepan, bring the heavy cream to a boil. Remove the saucepan from the heat, add the chocolate, and stir until the ingredients are combined. Allow to chill at room temperature for at least 3 hours.
2. Using a stand mixer fitted with a whisk attachment, whisk the frosting until light and fluffy.

Variations
+ If you are not a dark chocolate lover, you can replace it with the same amount of semi-sweet, milk, or white chocolate.

Savory Cream Cheese Frosting

Makes 1 cup

An easy rich frosting that turns any savory bake into a real treat.

Ingredients
1 cup (8 oz.) cream cheese
2 tablespoons heavy cream

Preparation
1. Using a stand mixer fitted with a whisk attachment, whisk the cream cheese and heavy cream.
2. Continue whisking until the mixture is light and fluffy.

Variations
+ Add two tablespoons of finely chopped basil, cilantro, or parsley.
+ Add ¼ cup of finely chopped red bell peppers, cucumbers, or green onions.

It's in the Filling

Lemon Cream & Meringue Cupcakes

These cupcakes offer a nice tangy lemon surprise with each bite. Remember that when a recipe calls for lemon zest, always grate before cutting the lemon. That way, if you don't need the juice, you can store the lemon in the fridge for later use.

Makes **48** cupcakes

Ingredients

5 eggs
1½ cups sugar
Zest of 1 lemon
2 sticks (8 oz.) butter, melted
1⅓ cups all-purpose flour
½ teaspoon baking powder

Lemon cream

6 egg yolks
1 cup sugar
½ cup fresh lemon juice +
zest of 1 lemon
2 sticks (8 oz.) butter
Swiss Meringue Frosting (see page 15)

Preparation

1. Preheat the oven to 350°F and line a mini cupcake pan with paper liners. Using a stand mixer fitted with a whisk attachment, whisk the eggs and sugar on high speed for about 5 minutes, until the eggs are fluffy and light. Reduce the mixer speed to medium and add the lemon zest and butter gradually.

2. Replace the whisk attachment with the paddle attachment and add the flour and baking powder gradually. Be careful not to overwork the mixture.

3. Spoon the batter into the cupcake cups, filling each about three-quarters full. Bake for 15 to 17 minutes, or until a toothpick inserted in the center comes out clean.

4. Transfer the pan to a wire rack and let the cupcakes cool to room temperature.

5. Make the lemon cream: Place the egg yolks, sugar, lemon juice, and lemon zest in a heatproof bowl. Set the bowl over a saucepan of gently simmering water and stir the mixture occasionally, until the sugar dissolves and the mixture has thickened, about 10 minutes. Remove the bowl from the pan.

6. Gradually add the butter while stirring, until the mixture is smooth. Refrigerate for at least 2 hours.

7. Transfer the chilled filling to a piping bag fitted with a round tip, or to a squeeze bottle. Insert the tip into center of each cupcake and pipe in about 1 teaspoon of filling.

8. Frost the cupcakes and serve them immediately, or store in an airtight container and refrigerate for up to 2 days.

Strawberry Surprise Cupcakes

Try these mini strawberry shortcakes when you feel the first signs of summer. That's the time to enjoy the freshest, sweetest strawberries of the year.

Makes **48** cupcakes

Ingredients

2 sticks (8 oz.) butter
1½ cups sugar
3 eggs
1½ cups flour, sifted
1 teaspoon baking powder
½ cup ground almonds
1 cup Crème Fraiche (see page 14)
1 cup strawberry jam

Strawberry meringue frosting
1 cup egg whites
(from about 8 large eggs)
1¾ cups sugar
½ cup strawberry jam
½ cup fresh strawberries,
tops removed and sliced

Preparation

1. Preheat the oven to 350°F and line a mini cupcake pan with paper liners. Using a stand mixer fitted with a paddle attachment, mix the butter and sugar on high speed for 5 minutes until the butter is fluffy and light. Add the eggs one by one, mixing after each addition.

2. In a medium bowl, mix the flour, baking powder, and ground almonds. Add the flour mixture and crème fraiche alternately to the mixer, and mix on medium speed until mixture is smooth.

3. Spoon the batter into the cupcake cups, filling each half full. Spoon a teaspoon of strawberry jam onto the batter in the cups and then top each with the remaining batter.

4. Bake for 15 to 17 minutes, or until a toothpick inserted in the center comes out clean.

5. Transfer the pan to a wire rack and let the cupcakes cool to room temperature.

6. Make the strawberry meringue frosting: Place the egg whites and sugar in a heatproof bowl. Set the bowl over a saucepan of gently simmering water and stir occasionally, until the sugar dissolves. Remove the bowl from the pan.

7. Using a stand mixer fitted with a whisk attachment, place the egg white and sugar mixture in the bowl and whisk until the egg whites have cooled and become firm.

8. Fold in the strawberry jam. Transfer to a piping bag and decorate as desired. Decorate the finished cupcakes with fresh strawberry slices.

Vanilla Cream & Meringue Cupcakes

A classic cupcake that will make chocolate lovers envious. It's an elegant yet fun treat that appeals to both a mature crowd and the younger bunch.

Makes **48** cupcakes

Ingredients

2 sticks (8 oz.) butter
1½ cups sugar
2 teaspoons vanilla extract
3 eggs
1½ cups all-purpose flour
1 teaspoon baking powder
½ cup ground almonds
1 cup Crème Fraiche (see page 14)
2 cups Pastry Cream (see page 14)
Swiss Meringue Frosting (see page 15)

Preparation

1. Preheat the oven to 350°F and line a mini cupcake pan with paper liners.

2. Using a stand mixer fitted with a whisk attachment, mix the butter, sugar, and vanilla extract on medium speed until the mixture has a creamlike texture.

3. Add the eggs one by one, mixing after each addition. Use a spatula to scrape the batter from the sides of the mixing bowl so that all the ingredients are incorporated.

4. In a separate medium bowl, mix the flour, baking powder, and ground almonds.

5. Add the flour mixture and crème fraiche alternately to the mixer, and mix on medium speed until mixture is smooth.

6. Spoon the batter into the cupcake cups, filling each about three-quarters full.

7. Bake for 15 to 17 minutes, or until a toothpick inserted in the center comes out clean.

8. Transfer the pan to a wire rack and let the cupcakes cool to room temperature.

9. Transfer the pastry cream to a piping bag fitted with a round tip, or to a squeeze bottle. Insert the tip into the center of each cupcake and pipe in about 1 teaspoon of filling.

10. Frost the cupcakes and serve them immediately, or store in an airtight container and refrigerate for up to 2 days.

Royal Raspberry Cupcakes

Before decorating these cupcakes with fresh raspberries, I put the berries in the freezer for 5 minutes to develop a beautiful frost and take on a candy-like texture.

Makes **48** cupcakes

Ingredients

2 sticks (8 oz.) butter
1½ cups sugar
3 eggs
1½ cups flour, sifted
1 teaspoon baking powder
½ cup ground almonds
1 cup Crème Fraiche (see page 14)
1 cup raspberry jam

Raspberry meringue frosting
1 cup egg whites
(from about 8 large eggs)
1¾ cups sugar
½ cup raspberry jam
½ cup fresh raspberries

Preparation

1. Preheat the oven to 350°F and line a mini cupcake pan with paper liners. Using a stand mixer fitted with a paddle attachment, mix the butter and sugar on high speed for 5 minutes until the butter is fluffy and light. Add the eggs one by one, mixing after each addition.

2. In a medium bowl, mix the flour, baking powder, and ground almonds. Add the flour mixture and crème fraiche alternately to the mixer, and mix on medium speed until mixture is smooth.

3. Spoon the batter into the cupcake cups, filling each half full. Spoon a teaspoon of raspberry jam onto the batter and then fill the cups with the remaining batter.

4. Bake for 15 to 17 minutes, or until a toothpick inserted in the center comes out clean. Transfer the pan to a wire rack and let the cupcakes cool to room temperature.

5. Make the raspberry meringue frosting: Place the egg whites and sugar in a heatproof bowl. Set bowl over a saucepan of gently simmering water and stir occasionally, until the sugar dissolves. Remove the bowl from the pan.

6. Using a stand mixer fitted with a whisk attachment, place the egg white and sugar mixture in the bowl and whisk until the egg whites have cooled and become firm.

7. Fold in the raspberry jam. Transfer to a piping bag and decorate as desired. Decorate each cupcake with a raspberry and serve them immediately, or store in an airtight container in the refrigerator for up to two days.

Cappuccino Cupcakes

I poured this cupcake batter directly into little ceramic espresso cups to create a European café atmosphere. Try it yourself if you've got the cups at home.

Makes **48** cupcakes

Ingredients

2 sticks (8 oz.) butter
1¾ cups powdered sugar
4 eggs
⅓ cup cocoa
¼ cup boiling water
3 tablespoons coffee liquor
(such as Kahlua)
1½ cups all-purpose flour
½ cup ground almonds
1 teaspoon baking powder

Whipped cream frosting
1 cup heavy cream
⅓ cup powdered sugar

Preparation

1. Preheat the oven to 350°F and line a mini cupcake pan with paper liners.

2. Using a stand mixer fitted with a whisk attachment, mix the butter and powdered sugar on medium speed until the mixture has a creamlike texture.

3. Add the eggs one by one, mixing after each addition. Use a spatula to wipe down the sides of the mixing bowl so that all the ingredients are incorporated.

4. In a small bowl, mix the cacao, boiling water, and coffee liquor.

5. Gradually add the cacao and liquor mixture to the batter.

6. Gradually add the all-purpose flour, ground almonds, and baking powder to the batter.

7. Spoon the batter into the cupcake cups, filling each about three-quarters full.

8. Bake for 15 to 17 minutes, or until a toothpick inserted in the center comes out clean.

9. Transfer the pan to a wire rack and let the cupcakes cool to room temperature.

10. Make the whipped cream frosting: Using a stand mixer fitted with a whisk attachment, whip the cream and powdered sugar together until firm, with a whipped cream consistency.

11. Frost the cupcakes with whipped cream and serve them immediately, or store in an airtight container and refrigerate for up to 2 days.

Passion Fruit Cupcakes

Passion fruit is available in specialty supermarkets. When ripe, it has a wrinkled and dimpled purple skin. To use it in this recipe, simply cut the fruit in half and spoon out the pulp. The seeds, which are edible, should be strained in a non-aluminum sieve.

Makes **48** cupcakes

Ingredients

2 sticks (8 oz.) butter
1½ cups sugar
Zest of 1 lemon
3 eggs
1½ cups all-purpose flour
1 teaspoon baking powder
½ cup ground almonds
1 cup Crème Fraiche (see page 14)

Passion fruit cream filling
8 egg yolks
½ cup passion fruit juice
(from about 10 passion fruits)
1 cup sugar
1½ sticks (6 oz.) butter

Preparation

1. Preheat the oven to 350°F and line a mini cupcake pan with paper liners.

2. Using a stand mixer fitted with a whisk attachment, whisk the butter, sugar, and lemon zest for about 10 minutes on medium speed, until light in color and fluffy.

3. Add the eggs one by one, mixing after each addition. Use a spatula to wipe down the sides of the mixing bowl so that all the ingredients are incorporated.

4. In a small bowl, mix the flour, baking powder, and ground almonds.

5. Add the flour mixture and crème fraiche alternately to the mixer, and mix on medium speed until all ingredients are incorporated. (Do not over-mix).

6. Spoon the batter into the cupcake cups, filling each about three-quarters full.

7. Bake for 15 to 17 minutes, or until a toothpick inserted in the center comes out clean.

8. Transfer the pan to a wire rack and let the cupcakes cool to room temperature.

Passion fruit cream cheese frosting

1 cup (8 oz.) cream cheese

1 cup powdered sugar

2 tablespoons passion fruit juice
(from about 2 passion fruits)

1 tablespoon heavy cream

9. Make the passion fruit cream filling: Place the egg yolks, passion fruit juice, and sugar in a heatproof bowl. Set the bowl over a saucepan of gently simmering water and stir occasionally, until the mixture thickens (about 15 minutes). Remove the bowl from the pan. Gradually add in the butter and whisk until mixture is smooth.

10. Refrigerate the filling for at least 2 hours.

11. Transfer the chilled filling to a piping bag fitted with a round tip, or to a squeeze bottle. Insert the tip into the center of each cupcake and pipe in about 1 teaspoon of filling.

12. Make the passion fruit cream cheese frosting: Using a stand mixer fitted with a paddle attachment, mix the cream cheese and powdered sugar until combined. Add the passion fruit juice and heavy cream and continue mixing for another 2 minutes.

13. Frost the cupcakes and serve them immediately, or store in an airtight container and refrigerate for up to 2 days.

Mascarpone & Marsala Cupcakes

These Italian-inspired cupcakes are a great match for any home-cooked Italian meal.

Makes **48** cupcakes

Ingredients

Raisin filling
½ cup water
½ cup sugar
½ cup light raisins
¼ cup Marsala

Cupcakes
2 sticks (8 oz.) butter
1½ cups sugar
2 teaspoons pure vanilla extract
3 eggs
3 oz. white chocolate, melted
1½ cups all-purpose flour
1 teaspoon baking powder
½ cup ground almonds
1 cup Crème Fraiche (see page 14)

Mascarpone frosting
8 oz. mascarpone cheese
1 cup powdered sugar
Zest of 1 lemon

Preparation

1. Prepare the raisin filling a day ahead: In a small saucepan, heat the water and sugar and bring to a boil. Reduce the heat and cook until the sugar dissolves. Remove the pan from the heat and add the raisins and Marsala. Let it sit at room temperature overnight.

2. Preheat the oven to 350°F and line a mini cupcake pan with paper liners. Using a stand mixer fitted with a whisk attachment, mix the butter, sugar, and vanilla extract on medium speed until the mixture has a creamlike texture.

3. Add the eggs one at a time, mixing after each addition. Use a spatula to wipe down the sides of the mixing bowl so that all the ingredients are incorporated. Add the melted chocolate and continue mixing at medium speed. In a separate bowl, mix the flour, baking powder, and ground almonds.

4. Add the flour mixture and crème fraiche alternately to the mixer, and mix on medium speed until mixture is smooth. Spoon the batter into the cupcake cups, filling each about half-way full. Spoon a teaspoon of raisins (without syrup) into each cupcake and fill the cups three-quarters full with the rest of the batter.

5. Bake for 15 to 17 minutes, or until a toothpick inserted in the center comes out clean. Transfer the pan to a wire rack and let the cupcakes cool to room temperature.

6. Make the frosting: Using a stand mixer fitted with a whisk attachment, whisk the mascarpone cheese on medium speed for about 3 minutes, until light and fluffy. Add the powdered sugar and lemon zest and mix for another 3 minutes, until the mixture is blended. Frost the cupcakes, decorate with a few raisins, and drizzle the Marsala syrup on top. Serve immediately, or store in an airtight container and refrigerate for up to 2 days.

Pistachio & Cherry Marzipan Cupcakes

These fancy cupcakes are a perfect dessert for a cocktail or holiday party.

Makes **48** cupcakes

Ingredients

16 oz. marzipan
2 tablespoons pistachio paste
5 eggs
1 stick (4 oz.) butter, melted
3 tablespoons all-purpose flour
1 cup maraschino cherries

Mascarpone buttercream frosting
1 stick (4 oz.) butter
2 cups powdered sugar
¾ cup mascarpone cheese
1 tablespoon coffee liqueur
(such as Kahlua)

Preparation

1. Preheat the oven to 350°F and line a mini cupcake pan with paper liners.

2. Using a stand mixer fitted with a whisk attachment, mix the marzipan and pistachio paste on medium speed for about a minute.

3. Add eggs one by one, using a spatula to wipe down the sides of the mixing bowl so that all the ingredients are incorporated.

4. Add the melted butter and flour, and continue mixing on medium speed until all the ingredients are well combined.

5. Spoon the batter into the cupcake cups, filling each about half-way full. Place one cherry in each cup and fill it three-quarters full with the rest of the batter.

6. Bake for 15 to 17 minutes, or until a toothpick inserted in the center comes out clean.

7. Make the frosting: Using a stand mixer fitted with a whisk attachment, whisk the butter and powdered sugar on medium speed for about 3 minutes, until light and fluffy. Add the mascarpone cheese and coffee liqueur and mix for another 3 minutes, until the mixture is combined.

8. Frost the cupcakes with mascarpone frosting and decorate the top of each with a cherry. Serve immediately, or store in an airtight container and refrigerate for up to 2 days.

Nuts Galore Cupcakes

I chose walnuts, pecans, and macadamia nuts for this recipe, but you can substitute with any nut of your choice. Almonds, pistachios, and peanuts also work great here.

Makes **48** cupcakes

Ingredients

2 sticks (8 oz.) butter
1½ cups Demerara (raw cane) sugar
2 teaspoons pure vanilla extract
3 eggs
1½ cups all-purpose flour
1 teaspoon baking powder
½ cup ground almonds
1 teaspoon cinnamon
1 cup Crème Fraiche (see page 14)
Swiss Meringue Frosting (see page 15)

Filling
½ cup walnuts
½ cup pecans
½ cup macadamia nuts
1 teaspoon cinnamon
⅓ cup Demerara (raw cane) sugar

Preparation

1. Preheat the oven to 350°F and line a mini cupcake pan with paper liners.

2. Using a stand mixer fitted with a whisk attachment, mix the butter, sugar, and vanilla extract on medium speed until the mixture has a creamlike texture.

3. Add the eggs one by one, mixing after each addition. Use a spatula to wipe down the sides of the mixing bowl so that all the ingredients are incorporated.

4. In a separate bowl, mix the flour, baking powder, ground almonds, and cinnamon. Add the flour mixture and crème fraiche alternately to the mixer, and mix on medium speed until mixture is smooth.

5. Make the filling: Place all the ingredients in a food processor and process until the nuts are broke into small chunks (stopping before they are finely ground).

6. Spoon the batter into the cupcake cups, filling each about half-way full. Place one teaspoon of the nut filling into each cup and fill it three-quarters full with the rest of the batter.

7. Bake for 15 to 17 minutes, or until a toothpick inserted in the center comes out clean.

8. Transfer the pan to a wire rack and let the cupcakes cool to room temperature.

9. Frost the cupcakes and serve them immediately, or store in an airtight container and refrigerate for up to 2 days.

Apple & Poppy Seed Cupcakes

I've made this recipe with all different types of apples, but I always go back to my favorite, Granny Smith. There's something about its tartness that gives a nice contrast to the sweet cupcake base.

Makes  48 cupcakes

Ingredients

1 stick (4oz.) butter
1 cup sugar
3 eggs, separated
¾ cup all-purpose flour
¾ cup ground poppy seeds
½ cup Crème Fraiche (see page 14)
2 apples, peeled and roughly grated
Cream Cheese Frosting (see page 17)

Preparation

1. Preheat the oven to 350°F and line a mini cupcake pan with paper liners.

2. Using a stand mixer fitted with a paddle attachment, mix the butter and ¾ cup sugar on medium speed for about 5 minutes, until the mixture has a creamlike texture.

3. Add the egg yolks one by one, using a spatula to wipe down the sides of the mixing bowl so that all the ingredients are incorporated.

4. Using a stand mixer fitted with a whisk attachment, whisk the egg whites and ¼ cup sugar until the mixture is fluffy.

5. Fold the egg whites into the butter mixture. In a separate bowl, mix the flour and ground poppy seeds.

6. Add the flour mixture and crème fraiche alternately to the mixer, and mix on medium speed until mixture is smooth.

7. Add the grated apples and continue mixing for another minute.

8. Spoon the batter into the cupcake cups, filling each about three-quarters full. Bake for 15 to 17 minutes, or until a toothpick inserted in the center comes out clean.

9. Transfer the pan to a wire rack and let the cupcakes cool to room temperature. Frost the cupcakes with the cream cheese frosting. Serve immediately, or store in an airtight container and refrigerate for up to 2 days.

Tiramisu Cupcakes

The famous Italian dessert in mini cupcake form. What could be better?

Makes **48** cupcakes

Ingredients

2 whole eggs + 2 egg yolks
½ cup sugar
⅓ cup all-purpose flour
½ stick (2 oz.) butter, melted

Coffee syrup
¼ cup water
2 tablespoons sugar
⅓ cup finely ground instant coffee
2 tablespoons Marsala

Mascarpone frosting
1 cup (8 oz.) mascarpone cheese
½ cup powdered sugar
1 tablespoon Marsala
1 tablespoon finely ground coffee

Preparation

1. Preheat the oven to 350°F and line a mini cupcake pan with paper liners.

2. Place the eggs, egg yolks, and sugar in a heatproof bowl. Set the bowl over a saucepan of gently simmering water and stir occasionally, until the sugar dissolves. Remove the bowl from the pan.

3. Using a stand mixer fitted with a whisk attachment, place the egg and sugar mixture in the bowl and whisk until the eggs have cooled and become firm. Gradually fold in the flour and then the melted butter.

4. Spoon the batter into the cupcake cups, filling each about three-quarters full. Reduce the oven temperature to 320°F and bake for 15 to 17 minutes.

5. Meanwhile, make the coffee syrup: In a small saucepan, heat the water, sugar, and coffee over medium heat and bring the mixture to a boil. Remove the pan from the heat and add the Marsala.

6. Once the cupcakes are ready (and still hot in the pan), pour a teaspoon of syrup over each. Transfer the pan to a wire rack and let the cupcakes cool to room temperature.

7. Make the frosting: Using a stand mixer fitted with a paddle attachment, mix the mascarpone cheese and powdered sugar on medium speed for about 5 minutes, until light and fluffy. Gradually add the Marsala and coffee and mix for another 3 minutes, until the mixture is blended.

8. Frost the cupcakes and serve them immediately, or store in an airtight container and refrigerate for up to 2 days.

Dulce de Leche Cupcakes

A traditional Spanish milk-based sauce, dulce de leche can be found in specialty supermarkets. It can be substituted with butterscotch or caramel syrup, which are quite similar.

Makes **48** cupcakes

Ingredients

2 sticks (8 oz.) butter

1½ cups sugar

2 teaspoons pure vanilla extract

3 eggs

1½ cups all-purpose flour

1 teaspoon baking powder

½ cup ground almonds

1 cup Crème Fraiche (see page 14)

1 cup dulce de leche

Swiss Meringue Frosting (see page 15)

Preparation

1. Preheat the oven to 350°F and line a mini cupcake pan with paper liners. Using a stand mixer fitted with a whisk attachment, mix the butter, sugar, and vanilla extract on medium speed until the mixture has a creamlike texture.

2. Add the eggs one by one, mixing after each addition. Use a spatula to wipe down the sides of the mixing bowl so that all the ingredients are incorporated.

3. In a separate bowl, mix the flour, baking powder, and ground almonds.

4. Add the flour mixture and crème fraiche alternately to the mixer, and mix on medium speed until mixture is smooth.

5. Spoon the batter into the cupcake cups, filling each about three-quarters full.

6. Bake for 15 to 17 minutes, or until a toothpick inserted in the center comes out clean.

7. Transfer the pan to a wire rack and let the cupcakes cool to room temperature.

8. Transfer the dulce de leche to a piping bag fitted with a round tip, or to a squeeze bottle. Insert the tip into the center of each cupcake and pipe in about 1 teaspoon of filling.

9. Frost the cupcakes and serve them immediately, or store in an airtight container and refrigerate for up to 2 days.

It's in the Topping

Upside Down Apricot Cupcakes

A great fall recipe. You can substitute the dried apricots with any other dried, tangy fruit such as apples, plums or pears.

Makes **48** cupcakes

Ingredients

2 sticks (8 oz.) butter
1 cup brown sugar
3 eggs
1 cup all-purpose flour
1 teaspoon baking powder
1½ cups ground almonds
1 cup Crème Fraiche (see page 14)

Apricot syrup
¾ stick (3 oz.) butter
1 cup brown sugar
¼ cup maple syrup
½ cup water
Around 24 dried apricots

Preparation

1. Preheat the oven to 350°F and line a mini cupcake pan with paper liners. Using a stand mixer fitted with a paddle attachment, mix the butter and brown sugar on medium speed for about 5 minutes until the mixture has a creamlike texture and is light in color.

2. Add the eggs one by one, mixing after each addition. Use a spatula to wipe down the sides of the mixing bowl so that all the ingredients are incorporated. In a separate bowl, mix the flour, baking powder, and ground almonds.

3. Add the flour mixture and crème fraiche alternately to the mixer, and mix on medium speed until mixture is smooth.

4. Make the apricot syrup: In a small saucepan, heat the butter, sugar, maple syrup, and water on medium heat, until the butter has melted and the mixture has a syrupy texture. Add the dried apricots and continue to cook for about 3 minutes. Remove the pan from the heat and let the mixture cool to room temperature.

5. Drain the apricots (keeping the syrup), and cut each in half. Place one half in each of the cupcake cups. Spoon ½ teaspoon of syrup onto each of the apricot halves. Spoon the batter into the cupcake cups, filling each about three-quarters full.

6. Bake for 15 to 17 minutes, or until a toothpick inserted in the center comes out clean. Transfer the pan to a wire rack and let the cupcakes cool to room temperature. Once cooled, carefully remove the cupcakes and serve them upside down.

7. Serve immediately, or store in an air tight container in the refrigerator for up to two days.

Chestnut Cupcakes

Nothing signals the coming of winter more than roasted chestnuts. This recipe calls for chestnut flour and sweet chestnut spread, both of which can be found in specialty stores.

Makes  48 cupcakes

Ingredients

3 whole eggs

4 egg yolks

1¼ cups sugar

1½ cups ground almonds

¾ cup all-purpose flour

⅓ cup chestnut flour

8 egg whites

8 oz. store-bought sweet chestnut spread

Preparation

1. Preheat the oven to 350°F and line a mini cupcake pan with paper liners.

2. Using a stand mixer fitted with a whisk attachment, whisk the 3 whole eggs, 4 egg yolks, and ½ cup of sugar on medium speed for about 5 minutes. Gradually add the ground almonds, all-purpose flour, and chestnut flour and continue to mix until all ingredients are blended.

3. In the bowl of a stand mixer fitted with a whisk attachment, whisk the egg whites and ¾ cup sugar until the egg whites are soft and fluffy.

4. Gently fold the egg whites into the batter. Spoon the batter into the cupcake cups, filling each about three-quarters full.

5. Bake for 15 to 17 minutes, or until a toothpick inserted in the center comes out clean.

6. Transfer the pan to a wire rack and let the cupcakes cool to room temperature.

7. Frost the cupcakes and serve them immediately, or store in an airtight container and refrigerate for up to 2 days.

Gingerbread Cupcakes

These cupcakes are great any time of year, but I especially like making them for breakfast on cold fall mornings.

Makes **48** cupcakes

Ingredients

1 stick (4 oz.) butter
1 cup brown sugar
½ cup honey
3 eggs
1 cup all-purpose flour
1 cup whole wheat flour
1½ teaspoons baking powder
1 teaspoon ground ginger
1 teaspoon cinnamon
¾ cup Crème Fraiche (see page 14)

Royal orange icing
1 tablespoon orange juice
1 cup powdered sugar
3 oz. candied ginger, coarsely chopped

Preparation

1. Preheat the oven to 350°F and line a mini cupcake pan with paper liners.

2. Using a stand mixer fitted with a paddle attachment, mix the butter, brown sugar, and honey on medium speed for about 5 minutes, until the mixture has a creamlike texture and is light in color.

3. Add the eggs one by one, mixing after each addition. Use a spatula to wipe down the sides of the mixing bowl so that all the ingredients are incorporated.

4. In a separate bowl, mix both flours and the baking powder, ginger, and cinnamon.

5. Add the flour mixture and crème fraiche alternately to the mixer, and mix on medium speed until mixture is smooth.

6. Spoon the batter into the cupcake cups, filling each about three-quarters full.

7. Bake for 15 to 17 minutes, or until a toothpick inserted in the center comes out clean. Transfer the pan to a wire rack and let the cupcakes cool to room temperature.

8. Make the royal orange icing: Mix the orange juice and powdered sugar using a whisk until the mixture is smooth and creamy.

9. Decorate the cupcakes with the frosting and top each one with candied ginger.

Pineapple & Coconut Cupcakes

If you make these cupcakes in the early summer months, replace the canned pineapple with one cup of fresh pineapple cubes, and give thanks to Hawai'i for this exotic fruit!

Makes **48** cupcakes

Ingredients

1 stick (4 oz.) butter

1 cup sugar

3 eggs, separated

¾ cup all-purpose flour

¾ cup grated coconut

½ cup Crème Fraiche (see page 14)

Swiss Meringue Frosting
(see page 15)

1 cup canned pineapple cubes

Preparation

1. Preheat the oven to 350°F and line a mini cupcake pan with paper liners.

2. Using a stand mixer fitted with a paddle attachment, mix the butter and ¾ cup of sugar on medium speed for about 5 minutes, until the mixture has a creamlike texture and is light in color.

3. Add the egg yolks one by one, using a spatula to wipe down the sides of the mixing bowl so that all the ingredients are incorporated.

4. In a separate bowl, whisk the egg whites and ¼ cup sugar until the mixture is fluffy. Fold the egg whites into the butter mixture.

5. In a separate bowl, mix the flour and grated coconut. Add the flour mixture and crème fraiche alternately to the mixer, and mix on medium speed until mixture is smooth.

6. Spoon the batter into the cupcake cups, filling each about three-quarters full. Bake for 15 to 17 minutes, or until a toothpick inserted in the center comes out clean.

7. Transfer the pan to a wire rack and let the cupcakes cool to room temperature.

8. Frost the cupcakes with the Swiss meringue frosting, and top each one with pineapple cubes. Serve immediately or store in an airtight container and refrigerate for up to 2 days.

Mascarpone & Polenta Cupcakes

Polenta, the Italian word for cornmeal, was originally considered "poor man's food." One taste of these luscious cupcakes will make you wonder why.

Makes **48** cupcakes

Ingredients

2 sticks (8 oz.) butter

1½ cups sugar

Zest and juice of 1 lemon
(about ¼ cup juice)

3 eggs

½ cup cornmeal

2 cups ground almonds

1 teaspoon baking powder

Mascarpone buttercream frosting

1 stick (4 oz.) butter

2 cups powdered sugar

5 oz. mascarpone cheese

Preparation

1. Preheat the oven to 350°F and line a mini cupcake pan with paper liners.

2. Using a stand mixer fitted with a paddle attachment, mix the butter, sugar, and lemon zest on medium speed for about 5 minutes, until the mixture has a creamlike texture and is light in color.

3. Add the eggs one by one, mixing after each addition. Use a spatula to wipe down the sides of the mixing bowl so that all the ingredients are incorporated. Add the lemon juice and mix.

4. In a separate bowl, mix the cornmeal, ground almonds, and baking powder. Gradually add the cornmeal mixture to the batter and mix until all ingredients are combined.

5. Spoon the batter into the cupcake cups, filling each about three-quarters full. Bake for 15 to 17 minutes, or until a toothpick inserted in the center comes out clean.

6. Transfer the pan to a wire rack and let the cupcakes cool to room temperature.

7. Make the mascarpone frosting: Using a stand mixer fitted with a paddle attachment, mix the butter on medium speed for about 5 minutes, until light and fluffy. Gradually add the powdered sugar and mascarpone cheese and mix for another 3 minutes, until the mixture is blended.

8. Frost the cupcakes and serve them immediately, or store in an airtight container and refrigerate for up to 2 days.

Oreo Cookie Cupcakes

The perfect cupcake to make when you have a sudden urge to bake. Who doesn't have Oreo cookies in their cupboard? Be warned, however: they'll be gone before you know it.

Makes **48** cupcakes

Ingredients

3 sticks (12 oz.) butter
10 oz. Oreo cookies
1½ cups sugar
3 eggs
1½ cups all-purpose flour
½ cup ground almonds
1 teaspoon baking powder
1 cup Crème Fraiche (see page 14)

Whipped cream frosting
1 cup heavy cream
⅓ cup powdered sugar
24 Oreo cookies, halved
(not split horizontally)

Preparation

1. Preheat the oven to 350°F and line a mini cupcake pan with paper liners. Melt 1 stick (4 oz.) butter. Blend the butter and 4 oz. of Oreo cookies In a food processor until the cookies are crushed. Refrigerate the mixture for 30 minutes.

2. Using a stand mixer fitted with a paddle attachment, mix 2 sticks (8 oz.) of butter and the sugar on medium speed until the mixture is fluffy and light in color, about 10 minutes.

3. Add the eggs, one by one, mixing after each addition. Use a spatula to wipe down the sides of the mixing bowl so that all the ingredients are incorporated. In a separate bowl, mix the flour, ground almonds, and baking powder.

4. Add the flour mixture and crème fraiche alternately to the mixer, and mix on medium speed until all ingredients are incorporated. (Do not over-mix.) Place a teaspoon of the crushed Oreos into each cupcake cup.

5. Spoon the batter into the cupcake cups, filling each about three-quarters full. Bake for 15 to 17 minutes, or until a toothpick inserted in the center comes out clean.

6. Transfer the pan to a wire rack and let the cupcakes cool to room temperature.

7. Make the whipped cream frosting: Using a stand mixer fitted with a whisk attachment, whisk the heavy cream and powdered sugar until light and fluffy.

8. Frost each cupcake with the whipped cream and decorate each with an Oreo cookie half. Serve immediately, or store in an air-tight container for up to two days in the refrigerator.

Sticky Bun Cupcakes

The texture of these cupcakes resembles the stickiest, sweetest part of a cinnamon roll – the gooey center. Don't dare skip the pecans; they add the needed crunch!

Makes **48** cupcakes

Ingredients

2 sticks (8 oz.) butter
1 cup brown sugar
3 eggs
1 cup all-purpose flour
1¼ cups ground almonds
1 teaspoon cinnamon
1 teaspoon baking powder
1 cup Crème Fraiche (see page 14)

Maple glaze
½ cup pecans, coarsely chopped
1 cup maple syrup

Preparation

1. Preheat the oven to 350°F and line a mini cupcake pan with paper liners.

2. Using a stand mixer fitted with a paddle attachment, mix the butter and sugar on medium speed for about 5 minutes, until the mixture has a creamlike texture and is light in color.

3. Add the eggs one by one, mixing after each addition. Use a spatula to wipe down the sides of the mixing bowl so that all the ingredients are incorporated.

4. In a separate bowl, mix the flour, ground almonds, cinnamon, and baking powder. Add the flour mixture and crème fraiche alternately to the mixer, and mix on medium speed until mixture is smooth.

5. Make the maple glaze: Place ½ teaspoon of chopped pecans into each of the cupcake cups. Spoon on half a teaspoon of maple syrup.

6. Spoon the batter into the cupcake cups, filling each about three-quarters full.

7. Bake for 15 to 17 minutes, or until a toothpick inserted in the center comes out clean. Transfer the pan to a wire rack and let the cupcakes cool to room temperature.

8. Serve the cupcakes upside down and immediately, or store in an airtight container and refrigerate for up to 2 days.

Calvados Cupcakes

Calvados is an apple-based brandy with origins in France. I like to add a little more than is called for in the recipe and drizzle a bit more on top of each cupcake.

Makes **48** cupcakes

Ingredients

3 eggs
1 cup brown sugar
½ cup sugar
1¼ cups canola oil
2 cups all-purpose flour
½ cup whole wheat flour, sifted
1 teaspoon baking soda
1 teaspoon cinnamon
¼ teaspoon ground cloves
⅓ cup apple cider
3 tablespoons Calvados
3 apples, peeled and cut into
small cubes
½ cup walnuts, coarsely chopped

Cinnamon whipped cream frosting
1 cup heavy cream
½ cup powdered sugar
1 teaspoon cinnamon

Preparation

1. Preheat the oven to 350°F and line a mini cupcake pan with paper liners.

2. Using a stand mixer fitted with a whisk attachment, mix the eggs and both sugars on medium speed for about 5 minutes, until the mixture has a creamlike texture and is light in color. Gradually add the canola oil.

3. In a separate bowl, mix both flours and the baking soda, cinnamon, and ground cloves. Gradually add the dry ingredients to the batter in the mixer. Then add the cider and Calvados.

4. Add the apples and walnuts and mix on low speed for 30 seconds, until all the ingredients are incorporated.

5. Spoon the batter into the cupcake cups, filling each about three-quarters full.

6. Bake for 15 to 17 minutes, or until a toothpick inserted in the center comes out clean. Transfer the pan to a wire rack and let the cupcakes cool to room temperature.

7. Make the frosting: Using a stand mixer fitted with a whisk attachment, whisk the heavy cream until firm and fluffy, add the powdered sugar and cinnamon, and mix to incorporate the ingredients.

8. Frost the cupcakes and serve them immediately, or store in an airtight container and refrigerate for up to 2 days.

Spiced Honey Cupcakes

In Ancient Egypt, honey was used to sweeten cakes and cookies. Today, the addition of honey will produce some of the best cupcakes you've ever tasted.

Makes  **48** cupcakes

Ingredients

¾ cup water
1 Earl Grey tea bag
3 eggs
½ cup sugar
½ cup honey
¾ cup canola oil
2¼ cups all-purpose flour
1 teaspoon baking soda
1 teaspoon cinnamon
½ teaspoon ground cloves
½ teaspoon ground ginger
Pinch of ground nutmeg
1 cup Crème Fraiche (see page 14)

Cinnamon cream cheese frosting
1 cup (8 oz.) cream cheese
1 cup powdered sugar
1 teaspoon fresh lemon juice
1 tablespoon heavy cream
1 teaspoon cinnamon

Preparation

1. Preheat the oven to 350°F and line a mini cupcake pan with paper liners.

2. In a small saucepan, bring the water to boil. Remove the pan from the heat, add the tea bag, and allow the water to cool to room temperature. Remove the tea bag.

3. Meanwhile, using a stand mixer fitted with a whisk attachment, whisk the eggs, sugar, and honey for about 5 minutes on medium speed, until fluffy and light in color. Gradually add the canola oil and mix.

4. In a separate bowl, mix the flour, baking soda, cinnamon, cloves, ginger, and nutmeg. Add the flour mixture and crème fraiche alternately to the mixer, and mix on medium speed until all ingredients are incorporated. (Do not over-mix.)

5. Spoon the batter into the cupcake cups, filling each about three-quarters full. Bake for 15 to 17 minutes, or until a toothpick inserted in the center comes out clean.

6. Transfer the pan to a wire rack and let the cupcakes cool to room temperature.

7. Make the frosting: Using a stand mixer fitted with a paddle attachment, mix the cream cheese and powdered sugar until fluffy and light in color. Add the lemon juice, heavy cream and cinnamon, and mix to incorporate the ingredients.

8. Frost the cupcakes and serve them immediately, or store in an airtight container and refrigerate for up to 2 days.

Apricot Cupcakes

Plan ahead when making these delicious cupcakes to make sure the apricots have time to marinate. Prepare the marinade before you go to bed, and bake the cupcakes when you wake up.

Makes  48 cupcakes

Ingredients

2 cups water
1 cup sugar
10 oz. dried apricots
¼ cup powdered sugar
16 oz. marzipan
4 eggs
⅓ cup all-purpose flour
¾ stick (3 oz.) butter, melted

Cinnamon cream cheese frosting

1 cup (8 oz.) cream cheese
1 cup powdered sugar
1 teaspoon fresh lemon juice
1 tablespoon heavy cream
1 teaspoon cinnamon

Preparation

1. Prepare the apricots in advance: In a small saucepan, heat the water and sugar on high heat and bring to a boil. Remove the pan from the heat and add the dried apricots. Allow to marinate for at least 6 hours.

2. Preheat the oven to 350°F and line a mini cupcake pan with paper liners. In a food processor, mix the powdered sugar and marzipan until smooth. Add the eggs one by one, while mixing.

3. Add the flour and melted butter and pulse until all the ingredients are incorporated.

4. Drain the apricots. Chop half and add them to the batter. Mix with a hand whisk or spatula. Spoon the batter into the cupcake cups, filling each about three-quarters full.

5. Bake for 15 to 17 minutes, or until a toothpick inserted in the center comes out clean. Transfer the pan to a wire rack and let the cupcakes cool to room temperature.

6. Make the frosting: Using a stand mixer fitted with a paddle attachment, mix the cream cheese and powdered sugar until fluffy and light in color, add the lemon juice, heavy cream and cinnamon and mix to incorporate ingredients.

7. Frost cupcakes, decorate with remaining apricots and serve them immediately, or store in an airtight container and refrigerate for up to 2 days.

Crème Brulée Cupcakes

The French have a way with their creams, and this French dessert-turned-cupcake will not disappoint even your creamiest expectations.

Makes **48** cupcakes

Ingredients

2 sticks (8 oz.) butter

1½ cups sugar

3 eggs

1½ cups all-purpose flour

½ cup ground almonds

1 teaspoon baking powder

1 cup Crème Fraiche (see page 14)

Mouseline cream frosting

2 cups whole milk

1 vanilla bean, split lengthwise and scraped

7 eggs yolks

1 cup sugar

3 tablespoons cornstarch

3 tablespoons all-purpose flour

2 sticks (8 oz.) butter

Preparation

1. Preheat the oven to 350°F and line a mini cupcake pan with paper liners. Using a stand mixer fitted with a paddle attachment, mix the butter and sugar on medium speed until the mixture is fluffy and light in color, about 10 minutes.

2. Add the eggs one by one, mixing after each addition. Use a spatula to wipe down the sides of the mixing bowl so that all the ingredients are incorporated. In a separate bowl, mix the flour, ground almonds, and baking powder.

3. Add the flour mixture and crème fraiche alternately to the mixer, and mix on medium speed until all ingredients are incorporated. (Do not over-mix.) Spoon the batter into the cupcake cups, filling each about three-quarters full.

4. Bake for 15 to 17 minutes, or until a toothpick inserted in the center comes out clean. Transfer the pan to a wire rack and let the cupcakes cool to room temperature.

5. Make the frosting: In a large saucepan, bring the milk and vanilla bean to a boil over medium heat. Remove the pan from the heat and remove vanilla bean. In a separate bowl, mix the egg yolks, sugar, cornstarch, and flour.

6. Gradually pour ⅓ of the hot milk into the egg yolk mixture while stirring constantly. Pour the mixture back into the saucepan and stir. Pour the remained egg yolk mixture into the saucepan and thicken it over low heat for 5-7 minutes, stirring constantly.

7. Remove the pan from the heat and stir to reduce the temperature. Add the butter. Cover with plastic wrap and refrigerate for at least one hour. Frost the cupcakes and serve them immediately, or store in an airtight container and refrigerate for up to 2 days.

Cola Cupcakes

Cola lovers beware: you may become as addicted to these cupcakes as you are to the drink!

Makes **48** cupcakes

Ingredients

1 stick (4 oz.) butter, melted

¾ cup Coca-Cola

1 egg

½ cup Crème Fraiche (see page 14)

¾ cup all-purpose flour

½ cup ground macadamia nuts

2 tablespoons cocoa

¾ cup sugar

1 teaspoon baking powder

Whipped Ganache Frosting
(see page 18)

Preparation

1. Preheat the oven to 350°F and line a mini cupcake pan with paper liners. In a large bowl, mix the butter, Coca-Cola, egg, and crème fraiche.

2. In a separate bowl, mix the flour, macadamia nuts, cacao, sugar, and baking powder.

3. Add the dry ingredients to the cola mixture and mix until all ingredients are incorporated.

4. Spoon the batter into the cupcake cups, filling each about three-quarters full. Bake for 15 to 17 minutes, or until a toothpick inserted in the center comes out clean.

5. Transfer the pan to a wire rack and let the cupcakes cool to room temperature.

6. Frost the cupcakes and serve them immediately, or store in an airtight container and refrigerate for up to 2 days.

Lemon Meringue Cupcakes

The kitchen torch recommended for this recipe is a useful tool for anyone who loves to bake. It gives this cupcake a beautiful golden sheen. You can find kitchen torches at specialty cooking shops.

Makes **48** cupcakes

Ingredients

2 sticks (8 oz.) butter
1½ cups sugar
Zest of 1 lemon
3 eggs
1½ cups all-purpose flour
½ cup ground almonds
1 teaspoon baking powder
1 cup Crème Fraiche (see page 14)
Swiss Meringue Frosting (see page 15)

Preparation

1. Preheat the oven to 350°F and line a mini cupcake pan with paper liners. Using a stand mixer fitted with a paddle attachment, mix the butter, sugar, and lemon zest on medium speed until the mixture is fluffy and light in color, about 10 minutes.

2. Add the eggs one by one, mixing after addition. Use a spatula to wipe down the sides of the mixing bowl so that all the ingredients are incorporated.

3. In a separate bowl, mix the flour, ground almonds, and baking powder. Add the flour mixture and crème fraiche alternately to the mixer, and mix on medium speed until all ingredients are incorporated. (Do not over-mix.)

4. Spoon the batter into the cupcake cups, filling each about three-quarters full.
Bake for 15 to 17 minutes, or until a toothpick inserted in the center comes out clean.

5. Transfer the pan to a wire rack and let the cupcakes cool to room temperature.
Frost with Swiss meringue frosting and using a kitchen torch, lightly scorch the meringue.

6. Serve immediately, or store in an airtight container and refrigerate for up to 2 days.

Pavlova Cupcakes

Pavlova is a meringue-based dessert that originated in New Zealand. It is named for the Russian ballet dancer, Anna Pavlova, and is created here in cupcake form.

Makes  48 cupcakes

Ingredients

2 sticks (8 oz.) butter
1½ cups sugar
3 eggs
1½ cups all-purpose flour
½ cup ground almonds
1 teaspoon baking powder
1 cup Crème Fraiche (see page 14)
Swiss Meringue Frosting (see page 15)

Whipped cream frosting
1 cup heavy cream
⅓ cup powdered sugar
5 passion fruits, pulp removed

Preparation

1. Preheat the oven to 350°F and line a mini cupcake pan with paper liners.

2. Using a stand mixer fitted with a paddle attachment, mix the butter and sugar on medium speed until the mixture is fluffy and light in color, about 10 minutes.

3. Add the eggs one by one, mixing after each addition. Use a spatula to wipe down the sides of the mixing bowl so that all the ingredients are incorporated.

4. In a separate bowl, mix the flour, ground almonds, and baking powder. Add the flour mixture and crème fraiche alternately to the mixer, and mix on medium speed until all ingredients are incorporated. (Do not over-mix.)

5. Spoon the batter into the cupcake cups, filling each about three-quarters full. Bake for 15 to 17 minutes, or until a toothpick inserted in the center comes out clean.

6. Transfer the pan to a wire rack and let the cupcakes cool to room temperature. Meanwhile, using a teaspoon, spoon the meringue frosting onto a baking sheet lined with parchment paper. With the back of the spoon, make indentations in the frosting to create little "cups."

7. Bake the meringue in a 240°F preheated oven for about an hour. Make the whipped cream: Using a stand mixer fitted with a whisk attachment, whisk the heavy cream and powdered sugar until the cream is stiff.

8. Place a meringue "cup" on each cupcake. Then fill the cups with whipped cream and top with passion fruit pulp. Serve immediately.

Jelly Cupcakes

Don't waste any leftover jelly you have when making these cupcakes. Keep it in the fridge to serve as dessert once the cupcakes are out of sight.

Makes  **48** cupcakes

Ingredients

2 sticks (8 oz.) butter

1½ cups sugar

Zest of 1 lemon

3 eggs

1½ cup all-purpose flour

½ cup ground almonds

1 teaspoon baking powder

1 cup Crème Fraiche (see page 14)

1 package of powdered gelatin, such as Jell-O (your choice of flavors), prepared according to the instructions on the package

Preparation

1. Preheat the oven to 350°F and line a mini cupcake pan with paper liners.

2. Using a stand mixer fitted with a paddle attachment, mix the butter, sugar, and lemon zest on medium speed until the mixture is fluffy and light in color, about 10 minutes.

3. Add the eggs one by one, mixing after each addition. Use a spatula to wipe down the sides of the mixing bowl so that all the ingredients are incorporated. In a separate bowl, mix the flour, ground almonds, and baking powder.

4. Add the flour mixture and crème fraiche alternately to the mixer, and mix on medium speed until all ingredients are incorporated. (Do not over-mix.) Spoon the batter into the cupcake cups, filling each about three-quarters full.

5. Bake for 15 to 17 minutes, or until a toothpick inserted in the center comes out clean. Transfer the pan to a wire rack and let the cupcakes cool to room temperature.

6. Pour a tablespoon of jelly on each cupcake (or until it's full) and chill the cupcakes in refrigerator until the jelly is firm. Serve immediately.

Plum Crumble Cupcakes

The classic cobbler recipe has been adapted here for cupcakes that are just as scrumptious. You can replace the plums here with apples for a traditional treat or cherries for a richer dessert.

Makes **48** cupcakes

Ingredients

½ stick (2 oz.) butter
¼ cup sugar
2 tablespoons port or dry red wine
8oz. (about 3) plums, pitted and
cut into cubes

Crumble
½ stick (2 oz.) very cold butter
¼ cup brown sugar
¾ cup all-purpose flour
¼ teaspoon cinnamon

Preparation

1. Preheat the oven to 350°F and butter a mini silicon cupcake pan.

2. In a large skillet, heat the butter, sugar, and port or wine. Add the plums. Cook for 10 minutes, until the plums are soft. Set aside to cool to room temperature.

3. Meanwhile, using a food processor, pulse together all of the crumble ingredients until crumbs form.

4. Pour the plum mixture into each cupcake cup, filling them ¾ full. Fill the rest of the cup with the crumble.

5. Bake for 20 minutes, until the crumble turns golden. Serve warm.

Ricotta & Pine Nut Cupcakes

Ricotta and pine nuts, usually ingredients for savory dishes, offer a pleasant surprise in this sweet cupcake.

Makes  **48** cupcakes

Ingredients

2 sticks (8 oz.) butter
1½ cups sugar
Zest of 1 lemon
5 eggs, separated
8 oz. ricotta cheese
¼ cup all-purpose flour
5 oz. roasted pine nuts

Mascarpone frosting
8 oz. mascarpone cheese
1 cup powdered sugar
Zest of 1 lemon

Preparation

1. Preheat the oven to 350°F and line a mini cupcake pan with paper liners.

2. Using a stand mixer fitted with a paddle attachment, mix the butter, one cup of sugar, and the lemon zest on medium speed for about 5 minutes, until the mixture is fluffy and light in color.

3. Gradually add the egg yolks and then the ricotta cheese. Remove the mixture from the mixer bowl and transfer it to a clean bowl. Remove the mixer's paddle attachment and affix the whisk attachment. Whisk the egg whites with ½ cup of sugar until the mixture is firm. Gradually fold the ricotta mixture into the egg whites.

4. Fold in the flour and 4 oz. of the pine nuts until all ingredients are incorporated. Spoon the batter into the cupcake cups, filling each about three-quarters full.

5. Make the frosting: Using a stand mixer fitted with a whisk attachment, whisk the mascarpone cheese on medium speed for about 3 minutes, until light and fluffy. Add the powdered sugar and lemon zest and mix for another 3 minutes, until the mixture is combined.

6. Frost the cupcakes, decorate with the remained pine nuts, and serve them immediately, or store in an airtight container and refrigerate for up to 2 days.

New York Cheesecake Cupcakes

This cupcake-cheesecake combination will please just about everyone. It's a bite-size version of the familiar cheesy treat, sweetened but not to the point of overkill. Make them with the berry of your choice, or go for a berry mix for a real taste bud awakener.

Makes **48** cupcakes

Ingredients

1 stick (4 oz.) butter, melted
8 oz. graham crackers
¾ cup (6 oz.) cream cheese
5 tablespoons powdered sugar
1 egg
3 tablespoons sour cream
1 teaspoon pure vanilla extract
1 cup berries

Sour cream frosting
1 cup sour cream
¼ cup powdered sugar

Preparation

1. Preheat the oven to 350°F and line a mini cupcake pan with paper liners. Place the butter and graham crackers in a food processor and blend until the graham crackers are crushed. Refrigerate the mixture for 30 minutes.

2. Using a stand mixer fitted with a whisk attachment, whisk the cream cheese and powdered sugar until well combined, about 5 minutes. Gradually add the egg, sour cream, and vanilla extract and mix until all ingredients are incorporated.

3. Place a teaspoon of the crushed graham crackers into each cupcake cup. Place a berry on top of the crust. Spoon the batter into the cupcake cups, filling each about three-quarters full.

4. Reduce oven temperature to 320°F. Bake for 15 to 17 minutes, or until a toothpick inserted in the center comes out clean.

5. Make the sour cream frosting: In a large bowl, whisk the sour cream and powdered sugar until well combined.

6. Pour a tablespoon of frosting over each cupcake and bake again at 350°F for 5 minutes. Transfer the pan to a wire rack and let the cupcakes cool to room temperature. Serve immediately, or store in an airtight container and refrigerate for up to 2 days.

Pomegranate Vanilla Cupcakes

Pomegranates may be a lot of work to peel, but once you get to the seeds, you'll be truly delighted. Pomegranate Syrup is a great sweetener and a good staple to have in your pantry. It can be found in health food supermarkets.

Makes  48 cupcakes

Ingredients

2 sticks (8 oz.) butter
1½ cups sugar
2 teaspoons pure vanilla extract
3 eggs
1½ cups all-purpose flour
1½ teaspoons baking powder
½ cup ground almonds
1 cup Crème Fraiche (see page 14)
¼ cup pomegranate syrup
Swiss Meringue Frosting (see page 15)
2 cups pomegranate seeds
(for decoration)

Preparation

1. Preheat the oven to 350°F and line a mini cupcake pan with paper liners.

2. Using a stand mixer fitted with a whisk attachment, whisk the butter, sugar, and vanilla extract for about 5 minutes on medium speed, until light in color and fluffy.

3. Add the eggs one by one, mixing after each addition. Use a spatula to wipe down the sides of the mixing bowl so that all the ingredients are incorporated.

4. In a small bowl, mix the flour, baking powder, and ground almonds.

5. Add the flour mixture, crème fraiche and pomegranate syrup alternately to the batter, and blend until the mixture is smooth.

6. Spoon the batter into the cupcake cups, filling each about three-quarters full.

7. Bake for 15 to 17 minutes, or until a toothpick inserted in the center comes out clean.

8. Transfer the pan to a wire rack and let the cupcakes cool to room temperature.

9. Frost the cupcakes with the Swiss Meringue Frosting and decorate each with a few pomegranate seeds. Serve them immediately, or store in an airtight container and refrigerate for up to 2 days.

Nothing but Chocolate

Cream Cheese & Chocolate Volcano Cupcakes

These cheesy and chocolaty cupcakes aren't for the lighthearted. Only true chocolate lovers will appreciate their intense chocolate flavor.

Makes **48** cupcakes

Ingredients

6 oz. dark chocolate
3 oz. milk chocolate
2 sticks (8 oz.) butter
1¼ cups sugar
16 oz. cream cheese
5 eggs
¾ cups flour
¾ cup powdered sugar
1 teaspoon pure vanilla extract
Cream Cheese Frosting
(see page 17)

Preparation

1. Preheat the oven to 350°F and line a mini cupcake pan with paper liners.

2. Place the dark chocolate and milk chocolate in a heatproof bowl. Set the bowl over a saucepan of gently simmering water, and stir occasionally, the chocolate melts. Remove the bowl from the pan.

3. Using a stand mixer fitted with a whisk attachment, mix the butter and sugar on medium speed. Once the butter is fluffy, add half the cream cheese and continue mixing.

4. Add three eggs, one by one, followed by the melted chocolate and flour. Be careful not to overwork the batter.

5. Spoon the batter into the cupcake cups, filling each cup half full. Replace the whisk attachment with the paddle attachment, and in a clean bowl mix the rest of the cream cheese with the powdered sugar on medium speed. Add the vanilla extract.

6. Add the remaining two eggs, one by one, and mix on medium speed until the ingredients are combined.

7. Spoon the cream cheese mixture into the cupcake cups, over the chocolate, filling them to the top. Bake for 15 to 17 minutes, or until a toothpick inserted in the center comes out clean.

8. Transfer the pan to a wire rack and let the cupcakes cool to room temperature. Frost the cupcakes and serve them immediately, or store in an airtight container and refrigerate for up to 2 days.

Sacher-Torte Cupcakes

The Sacher-Torte is the most famous Austrian culinary specialty. The original version, made only in Vienna and Salzburg, is shipped all over the world. But why wait for the next air-mail package when you can make it yourself in cupcake form?

Makes **48** cupcakes

Ingredients

2 sticks (8 oz.) butter
1 cup sugar
5 eggs, separated
8 oz. dark chocolate, melted
¾ cup all-purpose flour
1 cup apricot jam

Chocolate glaze
1 cup heavy cream
10 oz. dark chocolate

Preparation

1. Preheat the oven to 350°F and line a mini cupcake pan with paper liners. Using a stand mixer fitted with a whisk attachment, mix the butter and ½ cup sugar on medium speed for about 5 minutes, until the mixture has a creamlike texture and is light in color.

2. Add the egg yolks one by one, mixing after each addition. Use a spatula to wipe down the sides of the mixing bowl so that all the ingredients are incorporated. Gradually add the melted chocolate and continue mixing for another minute.

3. In a separate bowl, whisk the egg whites and ½ cup sugar until the mixture is fluffy. Fold the egg whites into the chocolate mixture.

4. Gradually add the flour and continue mixing for another minute. Spoon the batter into the cupcake cups, filling each about three-quarters full.

5. Bake for 15 to 17 minutes, or until a toothpick inserted in the center comes out clean. Transfer the pan to a wire rack and let the cupcakes cool to room temperature. Spoon the apricot jam into a piping bag fitted with a round tip, or to a squeeze bottle. Insert the tip into center of each cupcake and pipe in about 1 teaspoon of filling.

6. Make the chocolate glaze: In a small saucepan, heat the heavy cream until it boils. Remove the pan from the heat. Place the chocolate in a large heatproof bowl and pour on the boiled cream. Stir to combine. Allow to chill 10 minutes.

7. Dip the cupcakes into the chocolate glaze and serve immediately, or store in an airtight container and refrigerate for up to 2 days.

Black Forest Cupcakes

The origin of these cupcakes is the southern German dessert known as Schwarzwälder Kirschtorte, which literally means "Black Forest cherry liqueur torte." This version leaves out the liqueur but retains all of the chocolaty goodness.

Makes  cupcakes

Ingredients

2 sticks (8 oz.) butter
1 cup sugar
5 eggs, separated
8 oz. dark chocolate, melted
¾ cup all-purpose flour

Whipped cream frosting
1 cup heavy cream
½ cup powdered sugar
3 oz. dark chocolate, grated
8 oz. maraschino cherries

Preparation

1. Preheat the oven to 350°F and line a mini cupcake pan with paper liners.

2. Using a stand mixer fitted with a paddle attachment, mix the butter and ½ cup of sugar on medium speed until the mixture is fluffy and light in color. Add the egg yolks one by one, mixing after each addition. Mix in the melted chocolate, and transfer the entire to a clean bowl.

3. Using a stand mixer fitted with a whisk attachment, whisk the egg whites with ½ cup of sugar until the mixture is firm. Gradually fold the chocolate mixture into the egg whites. Fold in the flour until all ingredients are incorporated.

4. Spoon the batter into the cupcake cups, filling each about three-quarters full. Bake for 15 to 17 minutes, or until a toothpick inserted in the center comes out clean. Transfer the pan to a wire rack and let the cupcakes cool to room temperature.

5. Make the frosting: Using a stand mixer fitted with a whisk attachment, whisk the heavy cream and powdered sugar until the mixture is firm.

6. Frost the cupcakes and decorate with the grated chocolate and cherries. Serve them immediately, or store in an airtight container and refrigerate for up to 2 days.

Snickers Cupcakes

Turn everyone's favorite snack bar into a mini cupcake and you'll have a winning dessert to serve at your next gig.

Makes **48** cupcakes

Ingredients

2 sticks (8 oz.) butter
1½ cups sugar
3 eggs
1½ cups all-purpose flour
½ cup ground almonds
1 teaspoon baking powder
¾ cup Crème Fraiche (see page 14)
½ cup peanut butter

Maple cream cheese frosting

1 cup (8 oz.) cream cheese
½ cup powdered sugar
⅓ cup maple syrup

Preparation

1. Preheat the oven to 350°F and line a mini cupcake pan with paper liners. Using a stand mixer fitted with a paddle attachment, mix the butter and sugar on medium speed until the mixture is fluffy and light in color, about 10 minutes.

2. Add the eggs one by one, mixing after each addition. Use a spatula to wipe down the sides of the mixing bowl so that all the ingredients are incorporated. In a separate bowl, mix the flour, ground almonds, and baking powder.

3. Add the flour mixture and crème fraiche alternately to the mixer, and mix on medium speed until all ingredients are incorporated. (Do not over-mix.) Add the peanut butter and mix for another minute.

4. Spoon the batter into the cupcake cups, filling each about three-quarters full. Bake for 15 to 17 minutes, or until a toothpick inserted in the center comes out clean. Transfer the pan to a wire rack and let the cupcakes cool to room temperature.

5. Make the frosting: Using a stand mixer fitted with a paddle attachment, mix the cream cheese and powdered sugar until combined. Add the maple syrup and continue mixing for another 2 minutes.

6. Frost the cupcakes and serve them immediately, or store in an airtight container and refrigerate for up to 2 days.

Chocolate Mayonnaise Cupcakes

The combination sounds a bit weird, but I promise there's nothing weird about the taste of these cupcakes. The frosting takes on a marzipan texture, so be creative and cut out any shape that comes to mind.

Makes **48** cupcakes

Ingredients

2 cups all-purpose flour
½ cup cacao
1 teaspoon baking powder
1 cup mayonnaise
1 cup Crème Fraiche (see page 14)
1¼ cups sugar

Chocolate frosting
¾ cup light corn syrup
16 oz. dark chocolate, melted

Preparation

1. Preheat the oven to 350°F and line a mini cupcake pan with paper liners. In a medium bowl, mix the flour, cacao, and baking powder.

2. In separate bowl, mix the mayonnaise, crème fraiche, and sugar. Gradually add the dry ingredients to the mayonnaise mixture. (Do not over-mix).

3. Spoon the batter into the cupcake cups, filling each about three-quarters full. Bake for 15 to 17 minutes, or until a toothpick inserted in the center comes out clean. Transfer the pan to a wire rack and let the cupcakes cool to room temperature.

4. Make the frosting: In a medium bowl, mix the corn syrup and melted chocolate until well combined. Let the mixture cool at room temperature for at least 3 hours.

5. Sprinkle a clean surface with cocoa and roll out the chocolate to ¼-inch thickness. Using a standard cookie cutter or shape of your choice, cut out decorations for the cupcakes.

6. Serve immediately, or store in an airtight container and refrigerate for up to 2 days.

Plum, Port
& White Chocolate
Cupcakes

Although this elegant dessert is best suited for a mature crowd, the hint of white chocolate will make everyone feel a bit younger with every bite.

Makes **48** cupcakes

Ingredients

4 oz. dried pitted prunes, cut into cubes

½ cup port wine

1¼ sticks (5 oz.) butter

¾ cup sugar

½ teaspoon pure vanilla extract

3 eggs

1 cup all-purpose flour

1 teaspoon baking powder

⅓ cup sour cream

4 oz. white chocolate, melted

Meringue frosting

½ cup egg whites
(from about 4 large eggs)

2 cups sugar

Preparation

1. Marinate the prunes in the port wine for at least 6 hours. Drain the prunes and reserve the marinade for the frosting. Preheat the oven to 350°F and line a mini cupcake pan with paper liners.

2. Using a stand mixer fitted with a whisk attachment, whisk the butter, sugar, and vanilla extract for about 5 minutes on medium speed, until light in color and fluffy. Add the eggs one by one, mixing after each addition. Use a spatula to wipe down the sides of the mixing bowl so that all the ingredients are incorporated.

3. In a small bowl, mix the flour and baking powder. Add the flour mixture, sour cream, and melted chocolate alternately to the mixer, and mix on medium speed. Add the drained prunes. Mix until all ingredients are incorporated (Do not over-mix.)

4. Spoon the batter into the cupcake cups, filling each about three-quarters full. Bake for 15 to 17 minutes, or until a toothpick inserted in the center comes out clean. Transfer the pan to a wire rack and let the cupcakes cool to room temperature.

5. Make the frosting: Place the egg whites and sugar in a heatproof bowl. Set the bowl over a saucepan of gently simmering water and stir occasionally, until sugar is melted. Remove bowl from pan. Using a stand mixer fitted with a whisk attachment, place the egg white and sugar mixture in the bowl and whisk until the egg whites have cooled and become firm. Fold in the plum marinade.

6. Frost the cupcakes and serve them immediately, or store in an airtight container and refrigerate for up to 2 days.

Banana & Triple Chocolate Cupcakes

The combination of banana and chocolate is a classic; the combination of banana and three kinds of chocolate is a stroke of genius.

Makes  48 cupcakes

Ingredients

2 sticks (8 oz.) butter
1 cup brown sugar
4 eggs
2 cups all-purpose flour
1 teaspoon baking powder
¼ teaspoon cinnamon
¼ teaspoon ground ginger
A pinch of ground nutmeg
1 cup Crème Fraiche (see page 14)
3 bananas, mashed
¼ cup milk chocolate, chopped
¼ cup white chocolate, chopped
¼ cup dark chocolate, chopped
Cream Cheese Frosting
(see page 17)

Preparation

1. Preheat the oven to 350°F and line a mini cupcake pan with paper liners.

2. Using a stand mixer fitted with a paddle attachment, mix the butter and brown sugar on medium speed until light and fluffy, about 5 minutes.

3. Add the eggs one by one, mixing after each addition. Use a spatula to wipe down the sides of the mixing bowl so that all the ingredients are incorporated.

4. In a separate bowl, mix the flour, baking powder, cinnamon, ginger, and nutmeg. Add the flour mixture and crème fraiche alternately to the mixer, and mix on medium speed until all ingredients are incorporated. (Do not over-mix.) Add the mashed bananas and chopped chocolate, and mix for another minute.

5. Spoon the batter into the cupcake cups, filling each about three-quarters full. Bake for 15 to 17 minutes, or until a toothpick inserted in the center comes out clean.

6. Transfer the pan to a wire rack and let the cupcakes cool to room temperature. Frost the cupcakes. Serve them immediately, or store in an airtight container and refrigerate for up to 2 days.

Chocolate Porcupine Cupcakes

Kids, and maybe even some adults, will get a kick out of the idea of turning a cupcake into a porcupine.

Makes **48** cupcakes

Ingredients

2 sticks (8 oz.) butter

1 cup brown sugar

3 eggs

1 cup all-purpose flour

1¼ cups ground almonds

1 teaspoon baking powder

1 cup Crème Fraiche
(see page 14)

3 oz. dark chocolate, melted

Whipped Ganache Frosting
(see page 18)

Preparation

1. Preheat the oven to 350°F and line a mini cupcake pan with paper liners.

2. Using a stand mixer fitted with a paddle attachment, mix the butter and brown sugar on medium speed until light and fluffy, about 5 minutes.

3. Add the eggs one by one, mixing after each addition. Use a spatula to wipe down the sides of the mixing bowl so that all the ingredients are incorporated.

4. In a separate bowl, mix the flour, ground almonds, and baking powder. Add the flour mixture and crème fraiche alternately to the mixer, and mix on medium speed until all ingredients are incorporated. (Do not over-mix.)

5. Fold a quarter of the batter into the melted chocolate. Spoon 1 teaspoon of the chocolate batter into the cupcake cups, and fill the cups about three-quarters full with the "white" batter. Using a toothpick, swirl the chocolate batter around to create a marbled look.

6. Bake for 15 to 17 minutes, or until a toothpick inserted in the center comes out clean. Transfer the pan to a wire rack and let the cupcakes cool to room temperature.

7. Spread whipped ganache frosting generously on each cupcake, and use a small icing spatula to "pull" the frosting upward to create the porcupine spikes. Serve immediately, or store in an airtight container and refrigerate for up to 2 days.

Chocolate Soufflé Cupcakes

There are few desserts more satisfying than a chocolate soufflé – except for maybe a few chocolate soufflé mini cupcakes.

Makes  48 cupcakes

Ingredients

⅓ cup heavy cream
6 oz. dark chocolate
4 eggs, separated + 2 egg yolks
3 tablespoons rum
⅓ cup sugar

Chocolate glaze frosting
1 cup heavy cream
10 oz. dark chocolate

Preparation

1. Preheat the oven to 350°F and line a mini cupcake pan with paper liners. In a medium saucepan, bring the heavy cream to a boil over high heat. Remove the pan from the heat and add the chocolate, mixing until well combined. Gradually add the six egg yolks and rum, and mix until the mixture is smooth.

2. Using a stand mixer fitted with a whisk attachment, whisk the egg whites and sugar until fluffy and firm.

3. Fold the egg whites gradually into the chocolate mixture. Spoon the batter into the cupcake cups, filling each about three-quarters full.

4. Bake for about 10 minutes. The outside should be baked thoroughly, with the inside still liquidy. Transfer the pan to a wire rack and let the cupcakes cool to room temperature.

5. Make the chocolate glaze: In a small saucepan, heat the heavy cream until it boils. Remove the pan from the heat. Place the chocolate in a large heatproof bowl and pour on the boiled cream, stirring to combine. Cool at room temperature for 10 minutes.

6. Dip the cupcakes into the chocolate glaze and serve immediately, or store in an airtight container and refrigerate for up to 2 days.

Mint & Chocolate Fondant Cupcakes

Use only the small, undamaged mint leaves when candying them for the beautiful decoration on these cupcakes.

Makes **48** cupcakes

Ingredients

2 sticks (8 oz.) butter
10 oz. dark chocolate
4 eggs, separated + 4 egg yolks
½ cup powdered sugar
½ cup all-purpose flour

Mint chocolate ganache frosting
2 cups heavy cream
5 mint sprigs
16 oz. dark chocolate

Candied mint leaves
1 egg, white only
½ cup sugar
1 cup mint leaves

Preparation

1. Preheat the oven to 350°F and line a mini cupcake pan with paper liners. Place the butter and chocolate in a heatproof bowl. Set the bowl over a saucepan of gently simmering water and stir occasionally, until the mixture is blended. Remove the bowl from the pan.

2. Using a stand mixer fitted with a whisk attachment, whisk the eight egg yolks (reserve egg whites in a separate bowl for later use) and powdered sugar on medium speed for about 7 minutes, until fluffy and light in color. Reduce the mixer speed and gradually add the melted chocolate and flour. Spoon the batter into the cupcake cups, filling each about three-quarters full.

3. Reduce oven temperature to 340 F°. Bake for about 10 minutes. The outside should be baked thoroughly, with the inside still liquidy. Transfer the pan to a wire rack and let the cupcakes cool to room temperature.

4. Make mint chocolate ganache frosting: In a medium saucepan, bring the heavy cream and mint to a boil. Remove the pan from the heat and allow to rest for 30 minutes. Drain and save the heavy cream and throw away the mint. Bring the heavy cream to a boil again. Remove the pan from the heat and add the chocolate. Stir until the chocolate has melted and mixture is smooth. Let cool at room temperature for at least 3 hours. Using a stand mixer fitted with a whisk attachment, whisk the cooled chocolate ganache until light and fluffy.

5. Make the candied mint leaves: Brush the mint leaves carefully with the egg whites and dip each leaf in sugar. Frost the cupcakes and decorate with the candied mint leaves. Serve immediately, or store in an airtight container and refrigerate for up to 2 days.

Orange & Chocolate Cupcakes

There are two types of people in the world: those who love the combination of orange and chocolate and those who need to try it. These cupcakes are for both.

Makes **48** cupcakes

Ingredients

2 sticks (8 oz.) butter
1¼ cups sugar
Zest of 1 orange
3 eggs
¾ cup all-purpose flour
½ cup orange juice
6 oz. dark chocolate, melted
3 oz. milk chocolate, melted

Orange cream filling
8 eggs, yolks only
1 cup sugar
½ cup orange juice
1½ sticks (6 oz.) butter, cubed
and softened

Orange cream cheese frosting
1 cup (8 oz.) cream cheese
1 cup powdered sugar
1 tablespoon orange juice
1 tablespoon heavy cream
Zest of 1 orange

Preparation

1. Preheat the oven to 350°F and line a mini cupcake pan with paper liners. Using a stand mixer fitted with a paddle attachment, mix the butter, sugar, and orange zest on medium speed until the mixture is fluffy and light in color, about 10 minutes.

2. Add the eggs one by one, mixing after each addition. Use a spatula to wipe down the sides of the mixing bowl so that all the ingredients are incorporated. Add the flour, orange juice, and melted chocolates. Mix for another 2 minutes. Spoon the batter into the cupcake cups, filling each about three-quarters full.

3. Bake for 15 to 17 minutes, or until a toothpick inserted in the center comes out clean. Transfer the pan to a wire rack and let the cupcakes cool to room temperature.

4. Make the orange cream filling: Place the egg yolks, sugar, and orange juice in a heatproof bowl. Set the bowl over a saucepan of gently simmering water and stir occasionally until the mixture thickens, about 15 minutes. Remove the bowl from the pan. Gradually add in the butter. Refrigerate the filling for at least 2 hours.

5. Transfer the chilled filling to a piping bag fitted with a round tip, or to a squeeze bottle. Insert the tip into the center of each cupcake and pipe in about 1 teaspoon of filling.

6. Make the orange cream cheese frosting: Using a stand mixer fitted with a paddle attachment, mix the cream cheese, powdered sugar and orange juice until combined. Add the heavy cream and orange zest and continue mixing for another 2 minutes.

7. Frost the cupcakes and serve them immediately, or store in an airtight container and refrigerate for up to 2 days.

Nutella Surprise Cupcakes

Nutella is the famous Italian sweet hazelnut and chocolate spread. It's sold in supermarkets and specialty stores.

Makes **48** cupcakes

Ingredients

2 sticks (8 oz.) butter
1½ cups sugar
2 teaspoons pure vanilla extract
3 eggs
1½ cups all-purpose flour
½ cup ground almonds
1 teaspoon baking powder
1 cup Crème Fraiche (see page 14)
1 cup Nutella

Nutella buttercream frosting

1 cup egg whites
(from about 8 large eggs)

2 cups sugar

2 sticks (8 oz.) butter, cubed
and softened

2 teaspoons pure vanilla extract
8 oz. Nutella

Preparation

1. Preheat the oven to 350°F and line a mini cupcake pan with paper liners.

2. Using a stand mixer fitted with a whisk attachment, mix the butter, sugar, and vanilla extract on medium speed for about 5 minutes, until the mixture is light in color and fluffy.

3. Add the eggs one by one, mixing after each addition. Use a spatula to wipe down the sides of the mixing bowl so that all the ingredients are incorporated. In a small bowl, mix the flour, ground almonds, and baking powder.

4. Add the flour mixture and crème fraiche alternately to the mixer, and mix on medium speed until all ingredients are incorporated. (Do not over-mix.) Spoon the batter into the cupcake cups, filling each about three-quarters full.

5. Bake for 15 to 17 minutes, or until a toothpick inserted in the center comes out clean. Transfer the pan to a wire rack and let the cupcakes cool to room temperature. Transfer one cup of Nutella to a piping bag fitted with a round tip, or to a squeeze bottle. Insert the tip into the center of each cupcake and pipe in about 1 teaspoon of filling.

6. Make the Nutella buttercream frosting: Place the egg whites and sugar in a heatproof bowl. Set the bowl over a saucepan of gently simmering water and stir occasionally, until the sugar dissolves. Remove the bowl from the pan.

7. Using a stand mixer fitted with a whisk attachment, place the egg white and sugar mixture in the bowl and whisk until the egg whites have cooled and become firm. Gradually add the butter cubes, vanilla extract, and Nutella, mixing until well combined. Frost the cupcakes and serve them immediately, or store in an airtight container and refrigerate for up to 2 days.

Brownie & Coffee Cupcakes

Coffee is a great flavor enhancer for brownies. You wouldn't be overdoing it to serve these delicious cupcakes with a cup of hot coffee.

Makes  **48** cupcakes

Ingredients

2 sticks (8 oz.) butter
8 oz. dark chocolate
4 eggs
1½ cups sugar
1 tablespoon pure vanilla extract
½ cup all-purpose flour

Coffee frosting
½ cup egg whites
(from about 4 large eggs)
1 cup sugar
2 tablespoons coffee liqueur
(such as Kahlua)

Preparation

1. Preheat the oven to 350°F and line a mini cupcake pan with paper liners.

2. Place the butter and chocolate in a heatproof bowl. Set the bowl over a saucepan of gently simmering water and stir occasionally, until mixture is combined. Remove the bowl from the pan.

3. Using a stand mixer fitted with a whisk attachment, whisk the eggs, sugar, and vanilla extract on medium speed for about 5 minutes, until fluffy and light in color. Reduce the mixer speed and gradually add the melted chocolate. Fold in the flour.

4. Spoon the batter into the cupcake cups, filling each about three-quarters full. Reduce oven temperature to 320 F° and bake for about 15 minutes.

5. Transfer the pan to a wire rack and let the cupcakes cool to room temperature.

6. Make the frosting: Place the egg whites and sugar in a heatproof bowl. Set the bowl over a saucepan of gently simmering water and stir occasionally, until the sugar dissolves. Remove the bowl from the pan.

7. Using a stand mixer fitted with a whisk attachment, place the egg white and sugar mixture in the bowl and whisk until the egg whites have cooled and become firm. Add the coffee liqueur and mix until combined.

8. Frost the cupcakes and serve them immediately, or store in an airtight container and refrigerate for up to 2 days.

Chocolate Raspberry Cupcakes

This combination of chocolate and raspberry is definitely a winning team. Try to use fresh raspberries, especially for the top decoration and you'll be rewarded with a sweet, tangy treat.

Makes  **48** cupcakes

Ingredients

2 sticks (8 oz.) butter
1¼ cups sugar
3 eggs
6 oz. dark chocolate, melted
3 oz. milk chocolate, melted
1½ cups all-purpose flour
1 teaspoon baking powder
6 oz. fresh raspberries
(if using frozen raspberries, they must be thawed and well drained)

Whipped Ganache Frosting (see page 18)

Preparation

1. Preheat the oven to 350°F and line a mini cupcake pan with paper liners.

2. Using a stand mixer fitted with a paddle attachment, mix the butter and sugar on medium speed for about 7 minutes until the mixture is fluffy and light in color.

3. Add the eggs one by one, mixing after each addition. Use a spatula to wipe down the sides of the mixing bowl so that all the ingredients are incorporated. Add the melted chocolates and mix until incorporated.

4. In a small bowl, mix the flour and baking powder.

5. Add the flour and baking powder into the chocolate batter and mix until well combined. Add 4 oz. of raspberries and mix for another minute.

6. Spoon the batter into the cupcake cups, filling each about three-quarters full.

7. Bake for 15 to 17 minutes, or until a toothpick inserted in the center comes out clean.

8. Transfer the pan to a wire rack and let the cupcakes cool to room temperature.

9. Frost the cupcakes with the Ganache and decorate with the remaining 2 oz. of raspberries. Serve them immediately, or store in an airtight container and refrigerate for up to 2 days.

It's got to be Savory

Pumpkin, Ginger & Cheddar Cupcakes

These savory cupcakes are best to make in the fall, when pumpkins are plentiful. As they bake, they will fill your house with one of the most pleasing aromas of autumn.

Makes  48 cupcakes

Ingredients

2 cups all-purpose flour

2 teaspoons baking powder

1 teaspoon salt

¼ teaspoon ground ginger

¼ teaspoon ground nutmeg

1 stick (4 oz.) butter, melted

2 eggs

½ cup canned pumpkin

½ cup Crème Fraiche (see page 14)

1 cup fresh pumpkin, coarsely grated

3 oz. cheddar cheese, grated

Savory Cream Cheese Frosting
(see page 18)

Preparation

1. Preheat the oven to 350°F and butter or grease a mini cupcake pan. (You can also use an ungreased silicon pan.)

2. In a large bowl, mix the flour, baking powder, salt, ginger, and nutmeg. In a separate bowl, mix the butter, eggs, canned pumpkin, and crème fraiche.

3. Gradually add the dry ingredients to the batter; then add the grated pumpkin and cheddar cheese.

4. Spoon the batter into the cupcake cups, filling each about three-quarters full. Bake for 15 to 17 minutes, or until a toothpick inserted in the center comes out clean.

5. Transfer the pan to a wire rack and let the cupcakes cool to room temperature.

6. Spread on the savory cream cheese frosting and serve the cupcakes immediately, or store in an airtight container and refrigerate for up to 2 days.

Spinach & Pine Nut Cupcakes

To toast the pine nuts, put them on an ungreased skillet and heat over a medium flame until golden. Make sure to put some pine nuts aside to use as a topping.

Makes  **48** cupcakes

Ingredients

2 tablespoons olive oil

1 onion, chopped

10 oz. fresh spinach, chopped
(if using frozen spinach, it must be thawed and well drained)

3 garlic cloves, minced

2 cups all-purpose flour

2 teaspoons baking powder

1 teaspoon salt

½ teaspoon ground black pepper

1 stick (4 oz.) butter, melted

2 eggs

4 oz. ricotta cheese

3 oz. mozzarella cheese, grated

½ cup toasted pine nuts

Savory Cream Cheese Frosting
(see page 18)

Preparation

1. Preheat the oven to 350°F and butter or grease a mini cupcake pan. (You can also use an ungreased silicon pan.)

2. Heat the olive oil in a medium skillet over high heat, and sauté the onion, spinach, and garlic for about 7 minutes, until the onions are translucent. Remove from the heat and allow to cool to room temperature.

3. In a large bowl, mix the flour, baking powder, salt, and pepper. In a separate bowl, mix the butter, eggs, and ricotta cheese.

4. Gradually add the dry ingredients to the batter; then add the sautéed spinach, mozzarella, and pine nuts.

5. Spoon the batter into the cupcake cups, filling each about three-quarters full. Bake for 15 to 17 minutes, or until a toothpick inserted in the center comes out clean.

6. Transfer the pan to a wire rack and let the cupcakes cool to room temperature.

7. Spread on the frosting and serve the cupcakes immediately, or store in an airtight container and refrigerate for up to 2 days.

Sun-dried Tomato & Basil Cupcakes

Top these savory cupcakes with fresh cherry tomatoes and basil for an added touch of color and flavor.

Makes  **48** cupcakes

Ingredients

1 cup all-purpose flour

¾ cup cornmeal

2 teaspoons baking powder

2 teaspoons salt

1 teaspoon sugar

1 stick (4 oz.) butter, melted

3 eggs

½ cup sour cream

1 cup sun-dried tomatoes, chopped

½ cup feta cheese

2 tablespoons fresh basil leaves, chopped

3 tablespoons pine nuts

Savory Cream Cheese Frosting (see page 18)

Preparation

1. Preheat the oven to 350°F and butter or grease a mini cupcake pan. (You can also use an ungreased silicon pan.)

2. In a large bowl, mix the flour, cornmeal, baking powder, salt, and sugar.

3. In a separate bowl, mix the butter, eggs, and sour cream. Gradually add the dry ingredients to the batter; then add the sun-dried tomatoes, feta cheese, basil, and pine nuts.

4. Spoon the batter into the cupcake cups, filling each about three-quarters full. Bake for 15 to 17 minutes, or until a toothpick inserted in the center comes out clean.

5. Transfer the pan to a wire rack and let the cupcakes cool to room temperature.

6. Spread on the frosting and serve the cupcakes immediately, or store in an airtight container and refrigerate for up to 2 days.

Eggplant & Tahini Cupcakes

Tahini is paste of ground sesame seeds common in Middle Eastern cooking and can be found in specialty supermarkets. It is the main ingredient in these tasty cupcakes with an ethnic twist.

Makes  48 cupcakes

Ingredients

1 medium eggplant

2 cups all-purpose flour

2 teaspoons baking powder

1 teaspoon salt

1 egg

1 cup Crème Fraiche (see page 14)

¼ cup raw tahini

4 oz. mozzarella, grated

½ cup fresh basil leaves, finely chopped

Savory Cream Cheese Frosting (see page 18)

2 tablespoons roasted sesame seeds

Preparation

1. Preheat the oven to 350°F and butter or grease a mini cupcake pan. (You can also use an ungreased silicon pan.)

2. Using a fork, make holes in the eggplant by stabbing it several times. Line a baking sheet with aluminum foil and bake the eggplant for about 40 minutes, until it has softened (turning it over several times during the baking process).

3. Remove the eggplant from the oven and let it cool to room temperature. Slice the cooled eggplant in two lengthwise and remove the flesh, discarding the skin. Chop the flesh.

4. In a large bowl, mix the flour, baking powder, and salt. In a separate bowl, mix the egg, crème fraiche, and tahini. Gradually add the dry ingredients to the batter; then add the eggplant, mozzarella, and basil.

5. Spoon the batter into the cupcake cups, filling each about three-quarters full. Bake for 15 to 17 minutes, or until a toothpick inserted in the center comes out clean.

6. Transfer the pan to a wire rack and let the cupcakes cool to room temperature. Spread on the frosting and top with sesame seeds. Serve the cupcakes immediately, or store in an airtight container and refrigerate for up to 2 days.

Leek & Onion Cupcakes

Serve these savory cupcakes as an appetizer next time guests come to dinner. Use real Italian Parmigiano-Reggiano for a truly memorable taste.

Makes  48 cupcakes

Ingredients

2 tablespoons olive oil

1 onion, finely chopped

3 leeks, white and green parts, sliced into thin rings

4 garlic cloves, minced

3 green onion stalks, white and green parts, sliced into thin rings + another ⅓ cup reserved

2 cups all-purpose flour

2 teaspoons baking powder

1 teaspoon salt

¼ teaspoon ground black pepper

¾ stick (3 oz.) butter, melted

1 egg

1¼ cups sour cream

4 oz. Parmesan cheese, grated

Savory Cream Cheese Frosting (see page 18)

Preparation

1. Preheat the oven to 350°F and butter or grease a mini cupcake pan. (You can also use an ungreased silicon pan.)

2. Heat the olive oil in a medium skillet over high heat, and sauté the chopped onion, leeks, and garlic for about 7 minutes, until the onions are translucent. Add the 3 sliced green onions and sauté for another minute. Remove from the heat and allow to cool to room temperature.

3. In a large bowl, mix the flour, baking powder, salt, and pepper. In a separate bowl, mix the butter, egg, sour cream, and Parmesan cheese.

4. Gradually add the dry ingredients to the batter, followed by the sautéed onion, leeks, and garlic. Mix until all ingredients are combined.

5. Spoon the batter into the cupcake cups, filling each about three-quarters full. Bake for 15 to 17 minutes, or until a toothpick inserted in the center comes out clean.

6. Transfer the pan to a wire rack and let the cupcakes cool to room temperature.

7. Spread on the frosting and decorate with the reserved sliced green onion. Serve the cupcakes immediately, or store in an airtight container and refrigerate for up to 2 days.

Kalamata Olives & Feta Cheese Cupcakes

The tasty ingredients of a Greek salad are the main feature of these bite-size bakes. Kalamata olives have a lot of "meat" on them and are a good choice for baked dishes.

Makes **48** cupcakes

Ingredients

3 tablespoons olive oil

2 red bell peppers, diced

1 orange bell pepper, diced

½ green chili pepper, diced

4 garlic cloves, minced

2 cups all-purpose flour

2 teaspoons baking powder

½ teaspoon salt

¼ teaspoon ground black pepper

1 teaspoon dried oregano

¾ stick (3 oz.) butter, melted

1 egg

1¼ cups Crème Fraiche (see page 14)

½ cup feta cheese

4 oz. Kalamata olives, pitted and finely chopped

Savory Cream Cheese Frosting (see page 18)

Preparation

1. Preheat the oven to 350°F and butter or grease a mini cupcake pan. (You can also use an ungreased silicon pan.)

2. Heat the olive oil in a medium skillet over high heat, and sauté the peppers and garlic for about 7 minutes, until the peppers have softened. Remove from the heat and allow to cool to room temperature.

3. In a large bowl, mix the flour, baking powder, salt, pepper, and oregano. In a separate bowl, mix the butter, egg, and crème fraiche.

4. Gradually add the dry ingredients to the batter; then add the sautéed peppers, feta cheese and olives. Spoon the batter into the cupcake cups, filling each about three-quarters full.

5. Bake for 15 to 17 minutes, or until a toothpick inserted in the center comes out clean. Transfer the pan to a wire rack and let the cupcakes cool to room temperature.

6. Spread on the frosting and serve the cupcakes immediately, or store in an airtight container and refrigerate for up to 2 days.

Cornbread Cupcakes

These yummy cornbread bites are best when served warm and topped with a scoop of fine quality butter.

Makes  **48** cupcakes

Ingredients

1½ cups all-purpose flour

1 cup cornmeal

2 teaspoons baking powder

½ teaspoons baking soda

⅓ cup sugar

1 teaspoon salt

¾ stick (3 oz.) butter, melted

1 egg

1 cup Crème Fraiche (see page 14)

3 oz. cheddar cheese, grated

¾ cup canned (drained) corn kennels, chopped

½ jalapeño pepper, chopped

Preparation

1. Preheat the oven to 350°F and butter or grease a mini cupcake pan. (You can also use an ungreased silicon pan.)

2. In a large bowl, mix the flour, cornmeal, baking powder, baking soda, sugar, and salt.

3. In a separate bowl, mix the butter, egg, crème fraiche, cheddar cheese, corn kennels, and jalapeño pepper.

4. Gradually add the dry ingredients to the batter and mix until all ingredients are combined.

5. Spoon the batter into the cupcake cups, filling each about three-quarters full.

6. Bake for 15 to 17 minutes, or until a toothpick inserted in the center comes out clean. Transfer the pan to a wire rack and let the cupcakes cool for about 10 minutes. Serve warm.

Mexican Cupcakes

Enhance any Mexican meal with this savory accompaniment. You can substitute the savory cream cheese frosting with guacamole or sour cream. And don't forget to put out the salsa.

Makes  48 cupcakes

Ingredients

2 tablespoons olive oil

1 cup (3-4) green onions, white and green parts, sliced into thin rings + another ⅓ cup reserved

½ green chili pepper, seeds removed and finely chopped

2 tomatoes, seeds removed and finely chopped

1 cup all-purpose flour

¾ cup cornmeal

2 teaspoons baking powder

1 teaspoon salt

1 teaspoon sugar

1 tablespoon fresh cilantro leaves, roughly chopped

1 stick (4 oz.) butter, melted

3 eggs

¾ cup Crème Fraiche (see page 14)

Savory Cream Cheese Frosting (see page 18)

Preparation

1. Preheat the oven to 350°F and butter or grease a mini cupcake pan. (You can also use an ungreased silicon pan.)

2. Heat the olive oil in a medium skillet over high heat, and sauté 1 cup of the green onions, the chili pepper, and the tomatoes for about 7 minutes. Remove from the heat and allow to cool to room temperature.

3. In a large bowl, mix the flour, cornmeal, baking powder, salt, sugar, and cilantro. In a separate bowl, mix the butter, eggs, and crème fraiche.

4. Gradually add the dry ingredients and sautéed tomatoes to the batter and mix until all ingredients are combined.

5. Spoon the batter into the cupcake cups, filling each about three-quarters full.

6. Decorate the topping with chopped green onion and serve on the side. Serve the cupcakes immediately, or store in an airtight container and refrigerate for up to 2 days.

Smoked Salmon & Chive Cupcakes

Nothing beats a bagel and lox brunch, but these savory cupcakes are an interesting and tasty variation on the familiar theme.

Makes  48 cupcakes

Ingredients

2 cups all-purpose flour

2 teaspoons baking powder

½ teaspoon salt

1 stick (4 oz.) butter, melted

1 egg

1¼ cups Crème Fraiche (see page 14)

6 oz. smoked salmon, chopped

¾ cup chives, chopped + another
¼ cup reserved

Savory Cream Cheese Frosting
(see page 18)

2 oz. salmon caviar

Preparation

1. Preheat the oven to 350°F and butter or grease a mini cupcake pan. (You can also use an ungreased silicon pan.)

2. In a large bowl, mix the flour, baking powder, and salt. In a separate bowl, mix the butter, egg, and crème fraiche.

3. Gradually add the dry ingredients, smoked salmon, and ¾ cup chives to the batter and mix until all ingredients are combined.

4. Spoon the batter into the cupcake cups, filling each about three-quarters full.

5. Bake for 15 to 17 minutes, or until a toothpick inserted in the center comes out clean. Transfer the pan to a wire rack and let the cupcakes cool to room temperature.

6. Spread on the frosting and decorate with the reserved chopped chives and salmon caviar. Serve the cupcakes immediately, or store in an airtight container and refrigerate for up to 2 days.

Zucchini & Walnut Cupcakes

You can experiment with this recipe by using yellow zucchini along with the green for an extra splash of color.

Makes **48** cupcakes

Ingredients

1 cup all-purpose flour

¾ cup cornmeal

2 teaspoons baking powder

2 teaspoons salt

1 teaspoon sugar

1 stick (4 oz.) butter, melted

2 eggs

1 cup Crème Fraiche (see page 14)

1½ cups zucchini, grated (with skin)

½ cup walnuts, coarsely chopped

3 oz. Parmesan cheese, grated

Preparation

1. Preheat the oven to 350°F and butter or grease a mini cupcake pan. (You can also use an ungreased silicon pan.)

2. In a large bowl, mix the flour, cornmeal, baking powder, salt, and sugar.

3. In a separate bowl, mix the butter, eggs, and crème fraiche.

4. Gradually add the dry ingredients, zucchini, walnuts, and Parmesan to the batter, and mix until all ingredients are combined.

5. Spoon the batter into the cupcake cups, filling each about three-quarters full. Bake for 15 to 17 minutes, or until a toothpick inserted in the center comes out clean.

6. Transfer the pan to a wire rack and let the cupcakes cool to room temperature.

7. Serve immediately, or store in an airtight container and refrigerate for up to 2 days.

Cheese Soufflé Cupcakes

Don't make these cupcakes in advance: put them in the oven when your guests arrive, serve them hot, and watch them disappear!

Makes **48** cupcakes

Ingredients

5 oz. Parmesan cheese, grated
1¼ sticks (5 oz.) butter
3 tablespoons all-purpose flour
1 cup whole milk
3 oz. blue cheese, crumbled
4 eggs, separated + 2 egg whites
½ teaspoon salt
¼ teaspoon ground black pepper
A pinch of ground nutmeg

Preparation

1. Preheat the oven to 350°F and butter or grease a mini cupcake pan thoroughly.

2. Sprinkle a generous amount of Parmesan cheese in each cup. Reserve about a quarter of the grated cheese for adding in the next step.

3. In a small saucepan, heat the butter over medium heat until it melts. Whisk in the flour, and continue whisking and cooking for about 3 minutes; then add the milk and whisk until the mixture thickens, around 3 minutes. Whisk in the blue cheese and remaining Parmesan and remove from the heat.

4. Allow the mixture to cool to room temperature; then add the four egg yolks and mix until well combined. Using a stand mixer fitted with a whisk attachment, whisk the six egg whites until firm.

5. Gradually fold the egg whites into the cheese mixture. Fold in the salt, pepper, and nutmeg until the ingredients are incorporated.

6. Spoon the batter into the cupcake cups, filling each about three-quarters full.

7. Increase oven temperature to 375 F°. Bake for about 10 minutes, until the soufflés don't jiggle when you shake the pan a bit. Serve immediately.

Leek, Mushroom & Thyme Cupcakes

These savory mini cupcakes are filled with great surprises, but the best surprise comes in the topping - made with goat cheese!

Makes **48** cupcakes

Ingredients

2 tablespoons + ⅓ cup olive oil

1 leek, using only white part, sliced into thin rings

4 oz. fresh mushrooms (any kind), quartered

2 garlic cloves, minced

1 tablespoon fresh thyme leaves

2 cups all-purpose flour

2 teaspoons baking powder

1 teaspoon salt

¼ teaspoon ground black pepper

¾ stick (3 oz.) butter, melted

1 egg

1¼ cups Crème Fraiche (see page 14)

4 oz. Parmesan cheese, grated

Goat cheese frosting

6 oz. goat cheese

½ cup sour cream

Fresh thyme leaves (for decoration)

Preparation

1. Preheat the oven to 350°F and butter or grease a mini cupcake pan. (You can also use an ungreased silicon pan.)

2. Heat the 2 tablespoons of olive oil in a medium skillet over high heat, and sauté the leek, mushrooms, garlic and thyme for about 7 minutes, until the leeks are translucent and the mushrooms are soft. Remove from the heat and allow to cool to room temperature.

3. In a large bowl, mix the flour, baking powder, salt, and pepper. In a separate bowl, mix the butter, egg, crème fraiche, Parmesan cheese and remaining olive oil.

4. Gradually add the dry ingredients to the batter, followed by the sautéed leek and mushrooms. Mix until all ingredients are combined.

5. Spoon the batter into the cupcake cups, filling each about three-quarters full. Bake for 15 to 17 minutes, or until a toothpick inserted in the center comes out clean.

6. Transfer the pan to a wire rack and let the cupcakes cool to room temperature. To make the frosting: In a large bowl, whisk together the goat cheese and sour cream. Continue whisking until the mixture is light and fluffy.

7. Spread on the frosting and decorate with the fresh thyme leaves. Serve the cupcakes immediately, or store in an airtight container and refrigerate for up to 2 days.

Time for Celebration

Halloween Cupcakes

The decorative sugar dough pumpkins in this recipe are quite easy to make. They also add to the Halloween spirit, so you shouldn't leave them out. More experienced sculptors can show off their skills with a spider web.

Makes **48** cupcakes

Ingredients

2 sticks (8 oz.) butter
1½ cups Demerara (raw cane) sugar
3 eggs
1½ cups all-purpose flour
1 teaspoon baking powder
½ cup ground almonds
1 teaspoon ground ginger
¼ teaspoon ground nutmeg
1 cup canned pumpkin
½ cup toasted pumpkin seeds, chopped
Royal Icing (see page 15)

Sugar dough pumpkins
¾ cup + 2 tablespoons sugar dough
Orange food coloring

Preparation

1. Preheat the oven to 350°F and line a mini cupcake pan with paper liners. Using a stand mixer fitted with a whisk attachment, whisk the butter and sugar for about 5 minutes on medium speed, until light in color and fluffy.

2. Add the eggs one by one, using a spatula to wipe down the sides of the mixing bowl so that all the ingredients are incorporated. In a small bowl, mix the flour, baking powder, almonds, ginger, and nutmeg.

3. Add the flour mixture, canned pumpkin, and pumpkin seeds, alternately to the mixer and mix on medium speed. Mix until all ingredients are incorporated. (Do not over-mix.) Spoon the batter into the cupcake cups, filling each about three-quarters full.

4. Bake for 15 to 17 minutes, or until a toothpick inserted in the center comes out clean. Transfer the pan to a wire rack and let the cupcakes cool to room temperature. Frost each cupcake with the royal Icing.

5. Make the sugar dough pumpkin decoration: Sprinkle powdered sugar or corn flour on your work surface to prevent the dough from sticking. Roll the sugar dough into a ball. Press a finger in the center to create a hollow, and pour in a few drops of orange food coloring. Close the ball and knead it from the outside in.

6. When a uniform orange color is achieved, make smaller balls, about 1 inch in diameter. Place them on work surface and press each lightly to create indentation. With the help of a kitchen knife or toothpick, mark evenly spaced lines from the top center to the bottom center. Finish by rolling out the green sugar dough ball into a thin rope and cut ¼ inch pieces. Attach one stem on each pumpkin and put one dough pumpkin on top of each cupcake. Serve immediately, or store in an airtight container and refrigerate for up to 2 days.

Christmas Cupcakes

The perfect cupcakes to make with the kids on Christmas morning. You take care of the batter and watch them enjoy carving out sugar dough trees.

Makes  48 cupcakes

Ingredients

2 sticks (8 oz.) butter
1½ cups sugar
3 eggs
1½ cups all-purpose flour
1 teaspoon baking powder
½ cup ground almonds
1 cup Crème Fraiche (see page 14)

Sugar dough topping
10 oz. sugar dough
Dark green food coloring

Preparation

1. Preheat the oven to 350°F and line a mini cupcake pan with paper liners.

2. Using a stand mixer fitted with a whisk attachment, whisk the butter and sugar for about 10 minutes on medium speed, until light in color and fluffy.

3. Add the eggs one by one, mixing after each addition. Use a spatula to wipe down the sides of the mixing bowl so that all the ingredients are incorporated. In a small bowl, mix the flour, baking powder, and ground almonds.

4. Add the flour mixture and crème fraiche alternately to the mixer, and mix on medium speed until all ingredients are incorporated. (Do not over-mix.) Spoon the batter into the cupcake cups, filling each about three-quarters full.

5. Bake for 15 to 17 minutes, or until a toothpick inserted in the center comes out clean. Transfer the pan to a wire rack and let the cupcakes cool to room temperature.

6. Make the sugar dough topping: On a well floured surface, roll the sugar dough out to a thickness of about ⅛". Using a cookie cutter or sharp knife, cut circles out of dough and place one on top of each cupcake.

7. Place the remaining sugar dough in a bowl and mix in the dark green food coloring. Roll the dough out to a thickness of about ⅛", and use a sharp knife to cut out four triangles, each about 2 inches high. Cut out three spikes in each triangle and then attach all the triangles together. Decorate each cupcake with the sugar dough tree.

8. Serve immediately, or store in an airtight container and refrigerate for up to 2 days.

Baby Shower Cupcakes

To be safe, I decorate these cupcakes with light blue and light pink dots. But if the mother-to-be has shared the secret, you may want to go with one color only.

Makes  **48** cupcakes

Ingredients

2 sticks (8 oz.) butter
1½ cups sugar
3 eggs
1½ cups all-purpose flour
1 teaspoon baking powder
½ cup ground almonds
1 cup Crème Fraiche (see page 14)

Sugar dough topping
8 oz. sugar dough
Light blue food coloring
Pink food coloring

Preparation

1. Preheat the oven to 350°F and line a mini cupcake pan with paper liners.

2. Using a stand mixer fitted with a whisk attachment, whisk the butter and sugar for about 10 minutes on medium speed, until light in color and fluffy.

3. Add the eggs one by one, mixing after each addition. Use a spatula to wipe down the sides of the mixing bowl so that all the ingredients are incorporated. In a small bowl, mix the flour, baking powder, and ground almonds.

4. Add the flour mixture and crème fraiche alternately to the mixer, and mix on medium speed until all ingredients are incorporated. (Do not over-mix.)

5. Spoon the batter into the cupcake cups, filling each about three-quarters full. Bake for 15 to 17 minutes, or until a toothpick inserted in the center comes out clean. Transfer the pan to a wire rack and let the cupcakes cool to room temperature.

6. Make sugar dough topping: On a well floured surface, roll the sugar dough out to a thickness of about ⅛". Use a cookie cutter or sharp knife to cut circles out of dough, and place one on top of each cupcake.

7. Divide the remaining sugar dough into two balls. Mix the light blue food coloring into one and the pink food coloring into the other. Using your fingers, make small polka dots out of each color and decorate the cupcakes with the dots. Serve immediately, or store in an airtight container and refrigerate for up to 2 days.

Passover Cupcakes

From the taste, you'd never know these cupcakes are gluten-free. Make them year-round for people who are allergic to flour.

Makes  48 cupcakes

Ingredients

2 sticks (8 oz.) butter
¾ cup sugar
6 eggs, separated
8 oz. dark chocolate, melted
½ cup ground almonds
½ cup raspberry jam

Preparation

1. Preheat the oven to 350°F and line a mini cupcake pan with paper liners. Using a stand mixer fitted with a whisk attachment, whisk the butter and ½ cup of sugar for about 5 minutes on medium speed, until light in color and fluffy.

2. Add the egg yolks one at a time, mixing after each addition. Use a spatula to wipe down the sides of the mixing bowl so that all the ingredients are incorporated. Add the melted chocolate and continue mixing until the ingredients are combined.

3. Using a stand mixer fitted with a whisk attachment, whisk the egg whites and ¼ cup sugar until fluffy and firm. Gradually fold the egg whites into the chocolate batter, add the ground almonds, and fold until all ingredients are incorporated.

4. Spoon the batter into the cupcake cups, filling each about three-quarters full. Bake for 15 to 17 minutes, or until a toothpick inserted in the center comes out clean.

5. Transfer the pan to a wire rack and let the cupcakes cool to room temperature. Decorate each cupcake with a teaspoon of jam before serving.

Thanksgiving Cupcakes

The captivating aroma that fills your house as these cupcakes bake will convince you to make them more than once a year.

Makes **48** cupcakes

Ingredients

2 sticks (8 oz.) butter
1 cup sugar
½ cup brown sugar
3 eggs
2 cups all-purpose flour
1½ teaspoons baking powder
½ teaspoon ground ginger
1 teaspoon cinnamon
A pinch of ground cloves
1 cup canned pumpkin
½ cup fresh pumpkin, grated
Royal Icing (see page 15)

Preparation

1. Preheat the oven to 350°F and line a mini cupcake pan with paper liners.

2. Using a stand mixer fitted with a whisk attachment, whisk the butter and sugars for about 10 minutes on medium speed, until light in color and fluffy.

3. Add the eggs one by one, mixing after each addition. Use a spatula to wipe down the sides of the mixing bowl so that all the ingredients are incorporated.

4. In a small bowl, mix the flour, baking powder, ground ginger, cinnamon, and cloves. In a separate bowl, mix the canned pumpkin and fresh grated pumpkin.

5. Add the flour mixture and pumpkin alternately to the mixer on medium speed. Mix until all ingredients are incorporated. (Do not over-mix.) Spoon the batter into the cupcake cups, filling each about three-quarters full.

6. Bake for 15 to 17 minutes, or until a toothpick inserted in the center comes out clean. Transfer the pan to a wire rack and let the cupcakes cool to room temperature. Ice the cupcakes and serve them immediately, or store in an airtight container and refrigerate for up to 2 days.

Easter Egg Nest Cupcakes

These cupcakes are almost (almost) too cute to eat.

Makes  48 cupcakes

Ingredients

2 sticks (8 oz.) butter
1½ cups sugar
3 eggs
1½ cups all-purpose flour
1 teaspoon baking powder
½ cup ground almonds
1 cup Crème Fraiche (see page 14)

Sugar dough topping
10 oz. sugar dough
½ cup shredded milk chocolate or chocolate sprinkles
Light blue food coloring
Pink food coloring
Yellow food coloring

Preparation

1. Preheat the oven to 350°F and line a mini cupcake pan with paper liners.

2. Using a stand mixer fitted with a whisk attachment, whisk the butter and sugar for about 10 minutes on medium speed, until light in color and fluffy.

3. Add the eggs one by one, mixing after each addition. Use a spatula to wipe down the sides of the mixing bowl so that all the ingredients are incorporated. In a small bowl, mix the flour, baking powder, and ground almonds.

4. Add the flour mixture and crème fraiche alternately to the mixer, and mix on medium speed until all ingredients are incorporated. (Do not over-mix.) Spoon the batter into the cupcake cups, filling each about three-quarters full.

5. Bake for 15 to 17 minutes, or until a toothpick inserted in the center comes out clean. Transfer the pan to a wire rack and let the cupcakes cool to room temperature.

6. Make sugar dough topping: On a well floured surface, roll the sugar dough out to a thickness of about ⅛". Using a cookie cutter or sharp knife, cut circles out of the dough and place one on top of each cupcake.

7. Using the chocolate shreds or sprinkles, make a nest shape on each cupcake. Divide the remaining sugar dough into three balls and mix the light blue food coloring into one, the pink food coloring into the second, and the yellow food coloring into the third. Using your fingers, shape small eggs out of each color, and place them in the nests on each cupcake. Serve immediately, or store in an airtight container and refrigerate for up to 2 days.

Birthday Ice Cream Cone Cupcakes

To make marshmallows of different colors, just place them in separate bowls and add whatever food coloring you like.

Makes **48** cupcakes

Ingredients

2 sticks (8 oz.) butter
1½ cups sugar
3 eggs
1½ cups all-purpose flour
1 teaspoon baking powder
½ cup ground almonds
1 cup Crème Fraiche (see page 14)
48 small ice cream cones

Marshmallow topping

1 teaspoon gelatin + ¼ cup cold water
1¼ cups sugar
¼ cup light corn syrup
⅓ cup water
1 cup egg whites
(from about 8 large eggs)

Preparation

1. Preheat the oven to 350°F and line a mini cupcake pan with paper liners. Using a stand mixer fitted with a whisk attachment, whisk the butter and sugar for about 10 minutes on medium speed, until light in color and fluffy.

2. Add the eggs one by one, mixing after each addition. Use a spatula to wipe down the sides of the mixing bowl so that all the ingredients are incorporated. In a small bowl, mix the flour, baking powder, and ground almonds.

3. Add the flour mixture and crème fraiche alternately to the mixer, and mix on medium speed until all ingredients are incorporated. (Do not over-mix.) Spoon the batter into the cupcake cups, filling each about three-quarters full.

4. Bake for 15 to 17 minutes, or until a toothpick inserted in the center comes out clean. Transfer the pan to a wire rack and let the cupcakes cool to room temperature. Remove the cooled cupcakes from the paper liners, and place each one in an ice cream cone.

5. Make the marshmallow topping: In a small bowl, mix the gelatin and water until all the water is absorbed, about 10-15 minutes. In a medium saucepan over medium heat, mix the sugar, corn syrup, and water until the mixture reaches 220°F. Tip: If you don't have a kitchen thermometer, watch for when the bubbles become large and evaporate slowly. To be sure it's ready, remove a teaspoon of the mixture and place it in a cup filled with cold water. The syrup, when ready, will become solid.

6. Using a stand mixer with a whisk attachment, whisk the egg whites until firm. Gradually add the syrup mixture, whisking constantly. Add the gelatin and whisk until the mixture has cooled. Pipe the mixture onto each cupcake and refrigerate for at least an hour before serving.

St. Patrick's Day Cupcakes

It's customary to pinch anyone not wearing green on St. Patrick's Day. But why not just reward your green-clad friends at work with a gift of a St. Patrick's Day cupcake?

Makes  48 cupcakes

Ingredients

2 sticks (8 oz.) butter
1½ cups sugar
3 eggs
1½ cups all-purpose flour
1 teaspoon baking powder
½ cup ground almonds
1 cup Crème Fraiche (see page 14)
5 oz. sugar dough
Green-colored sugar

Preparation

1. Preheat the oven to 350°F and line a mini cupcake pan with paper liners.

2. Using a stand mixer fitted with a whisk attachment, whisk the butter and sugar for about 10 minutes on medium speed, until light in color and fluffy.

3. Add the eggs one by one, mixing after each addition. Use a spatula to wipe down the sides of the mixing bowl so that all the ingredients are incorporated.

4. In a small bowl, mix the flour, baking powder, and ground almonds. Add the flour mixture and crème fraiche alternately to the mixer, and mix on medium speed until all ingredients are incorporated. (Do not over-mix.)

5. Spoon the batter into the cupcake cups, filling each about three-quarters full. Bake for 15 to 17 minutes, or until a toothpick inserted in the center comes out clean. Transfer the pan to a wire rack and let the cupcakes cool to room temperature.

6. Make sugar dough topping: On a well floured surface, roll the sugar dough out to a thickness of about ⅛". Using a cookie cutter or a sharp knife, cut circles out of the dough and place one on top of each cupcake.

7. Dip a small, clean paintbrush into water and draw a four-leaf clover on each cupcake. Sprinkle the green-colored sugar over the cupcake and it will stick to the areas painted with water. Serve immediately, or store in an airtight container and refrigerate for up to 2 days.

Valentine's Day Cupcakes

These simple, sweet cupcakes are the perfect way to tell your loved ones – husband, kids, parents, or anyone – that they deserve something special.

Makes  cupcakes

Ingredients

2 sticks (8 oz.) butter
1½ cups sugar
3 eggs
1½ cups all-purpose flour
1 teaspoon baking powder
½ cup ground almonds
1 cup Crème Fraiche (see page 14)
1 cup fresh raspberries
Royal Icing (see page 15)

Sugar dough topping
4 oz. sugar dough
Pink food coloring

Preparation

1. Preheat the oven to 350°F and line a mini cupcake pan with paper liners.

2. Using a stand mixer fitted with a whisk attachment, whisk the butter and sugar for about 10 minutes on medium speed, until light in color and fluffy.

3. Add the eggs one by one, mixing after each addition. Use a spatula to wipe down the sides of the mixing bowl so that all the ingredients are incorporated. In a small bowl, mix the flour, baking powder, and ground almonds.

4. Add the flour mixture and crème fraiche alternately to the mixer, and mix on medium speed until all ingredients are incorporated. (Do not over-mix.) Add the raspberries and mix for another minute.

5. Spoon the batter into the cupcake cups, filling each about three-quarters full. Bake for 15 to 17 minutes, or until a toothpick inserted in the center comes out clean.

6. Transfer the pan to a wire rack and let the cupcakes cool to room temperature.

7. Make sugar dough topping: Mix the sugar dough with a small amount of food coloring, until you reach the desired color. On a well floured surface, roll the sugar dough out to a thickness of about ⅛". Using a sharp knife or heart-shaped cookie cutter, cut out 48 small heart shapes.

8. Ice the cupcakes and top each with a heart. Serve them immediately, or store in an airtight container and refrigerate for up to 2 days.

White Wedding Cupcakes

Cupcakes are the new wedding cakes. These elegant mini cupcakes can decorate the dessert buffet or be given out as party favors to your guests. Get really creative and use them as the base for your place cards.

Makes  48 cupcakes

Ingredients

2 sticks (8 oz.) butter
1½ cups sugar
2 teaspoons pure vanilla extract
3 eggs
1½ cups all-purpose flour
1½ teaspoons baking powder
½ cup ground almonds
1 cup Crème Fraiche (see page 14)
Pastry Cream (see page 14)
Swiss Meringue Frosting (see page 15)

Preparation

1. Preheat the oven to 350°F and line a mini cupcake pan with paper liners.

2. Using a stand mixer fitted with a whisk attachment, whisk the butter, sugar, and vanilla extract for about 5 minutes on medium speed, until light in color and fluffy.

3. Add the eggs one by one, mixing after each addition. Use a spatula to wipe down the sides of the mixing bowl so that all the ingredients are incorporated. In a small bowl, mix the flour, baking powder, and ground almonds.

4. Add the flour mixture and crème fraiche alternately to the batter, and blend until the mixture is smooth. Spoon the batter into the cupcake cups, filling each about three-quarters full.

5. Bake for 15 to 17 minutes, or until a toothpick inserted in the center comes out clean. Transfer the pan to a wire rack and let the cupcakes cool to room temperature.

6. Transfer pastry cream to a piping bag fitted with a round tip, or to a squeeze bottle. Insert the tip into center of each cupcake and pipe in about 1 teaspoon of filling.

7. Frost the cupcakes with the Swiss Meringue Frosting and serve them immediately, or store in an airtight container and refrigerate for up to 2 days.

Index

Conversion Charts

The recipes that appear in this cookbook use the standard United States method for measuring liquid and dry or solid ingredients (teaspoons, tablespoons, and cups). The information on this chart is provided to help cooks outside the U.S. successfully use these recipes. All equivalents are approximate.

METRIC EQUIVALENTS FOR DIFFERENT TYPES OF INGREDIENTS

A standard cup measure of a dry or solid ingredient will vary in weight depending on the type of ingredient. A standard cup of liquid is the same volume for any type of liquid. Use the following chart when converting standard cup measures to grams (weight) or milliliters (volume).

Standard Cup	Fine Powder (ex. flour)	Grain (ex. rice)	Granular (ex. sugar)	Liquid Solids (ex. butter)	Liquid (ex. milk)
1	140 g	150 g	190 g	200 g	240 ml
¾	105 g	113 g	143 g	150 g	180 ml
⅔	93 g	100 g	125 g	133 g	160 ml
½	70 g	75 g	95 g	100 g	120 ml
⅓	47 g	50 g	63 g	67 g	80 ml
¼	35 g	38 g	48 g	50 g	60 ml
¼	18 g	19 g	24 g	25 g	30 ml

USEFUL EQUIVALENTS FOR DRY INGREDIENTS BY WEIGHT

(To convert ounces to grams, multiply the number of ounces by 30.)

1 oz	=	1/16 lb	=	30g
4 oz	=	¼ lb	=	120g
8 oz	=	½ lb	=	240g
12 oz	=	1 lb	=	480g

USEFUL EQUIVALENTS FOR COOKING/OVEN TEMPERATURES

	Fahrenheit	Celsius	Gas Mark
Freeze Water	32° F	0° C	
Room Temperature	68° F	20° C	
Boil Water	212° F	100° C	
Bake	325° F	160° C	3
	350° F	180° C	4
	375° F	190° C	5
	400° F	200° C	6
	425° F	220° C	7
	450° F	230° C	8
Broil			Grill

USEFUL EQUIVALENTS FOR LENGTH

(To convert inches to centimeters multiply number of inches by 2.5.)

1 in					=	2.5 cm		
6 in	=	½ ft			=	15 cm		
12 in	=	1 ft			=	30 cm		
36 in	=	3 ft	=	1 yd	=	90 cm		
40 in					=	100 cm	=	1 m

USEFUL EQUIVALENTS FOR LIQUID INGREDIENTS BY VOLUME

¼ tsp							=	1 ml		
½ tsp							=	2 ml		
1 tsp							=	5 ml		
3 tsp	=	1 tbls				½ fl oz	=	15 ml		
		2 tbls	=	⅛ cup	=	1 fl oz	=	30 ml		
		4 tbls	=	¼ cup	=	2 fl oz	=	60 ml		
		5⅓ tbls	=	⅓ cup	=	3 fl oz	=	80 ml		
		8 tbls	=	½ cup	=	4 fl oz	=	120 ml		
		10⅔ tbls	=	⅔ cup	=	5 fl oz	=	160 ml		
		12 tbls	=	¾ cup	=	6 fl oz	=	180 ml		
		16 tbls	=	1 cup	=	8 fl oz	=	240 ml		
		1 pt	=	2 cups	=	16 fl oz	=	480 ml		
		1 qt	=	4 cups	=	32 fl oz	=	960 ml		
						33 fl oz	=	1000 ml	=	1 liter